kelvin curry

AF251154

I'm Telling the Truth

What You Didn't Know About God

CREATION HOUSE
A STRANG COMPANY

I'M TELLING THE TRUTH by Kelvin Dwan Curry
Published by Creation House
A Strang Company
600 Rinehart Road
Lake Mary, Florida 32746
www.creationhouse.com

Unless otherwise noted Scripture quotations are from the New American Standard Bible-\Updated Edition, Copyright © 1960, 1962, 1963, 1968, 1971, 1972, 1973, 1975, 1977, 1995 by The Lockman Foundation. Used by permission. (www.Lockman.org)

Scripture quotations marked niv are from the Holy Bible, New International Version of the Bible. Copyright © 1973, 1978, 1984, International Bible Society. Used by permission.

Scripture quotations marked nlt are from the New Living Translation Student New Testament New Believer's Bible. Copyright © 1996 Tyndale House Publishers, Inc.

Cover designer: Rachel Campbell

Library of Congress Control Number: 2008937222
International Standard Book Number: 978-1-59979-484-6
First Edition
08 09 10 11 12 — 987654321
Printed in the United States of America

Dedication

God

Daddy, You are my everything, my first love! Without You, Jesus, I am nothing and my life is meaningless. You have been by my side and have had my back through everything I've been through. I love you so much! Thank You, Lord, for simply using me as one of Your many vessels to share Your love with the world. This is for You, Daddy! I love You!

My wife, Melanie

Baby, you are my best friend next to Jesus. I never really believed in true love until God brought you into my life. You are without a doubt a special gift of the Lord. Not to sound "corny" or anything but I love our love! (smile) You have supported me in everything and I can't imagine doing what I do without your encouragement. Thank you for your consistent love for me throughout the years. You are my soul mate. I love you, Mel!

My father, Jesse

Dad, you are the one who always told us that we could do anything we set our minds to. Thank you for this type of encouragement and for your generosity that you have given us since birth! Dad, thank you for the sacrifices that you made to raise us and for always being there for me whenever I really needed you. I love you, Dad!

In loving memory to my grandmother
Dorothy Fay Curry

I also dedicate this book to my "Granny" who has since gone on to be with the Lord. If she were still here, this is what I would tell her:

Granny, I still remember those visits to Los Angeles with you and Papa while you taped your Christian Radio Broadcast, *This is the Day That the Lord Has Made, I Will Rejoice and Be Glad In It*, in your bathroom. I have memories of my brother, Kevin, my cousin, Danielle, and me, listening to you record your messages as we played in the backyard. I believe that this work, along with your prayers for our whole family, planted a seed early on for me. Thank you, Granny, for being the glue and backbone that held the family together. I also want to thank you for the many talks that you had with us at your kitchen table and for your godly influence that is still impacting me today. I love you, Granny!

My children

You are special and dear to me. I dedicate this book to you all as well because you are the next generation. The greatest gift I could give you as your father is the gift of connecting you to Jesus. Take this word of God's love to heart and share it with the world. Do all that God has put in your heart to do and stay committed to the call. I love you all so very much! Daddy.

Contents

Kelvin's Prayer

I'm Trying to Reach a Generation
I'm trying to reach a generation that don't look like you or me
I'm trying to reach a generation that's in bondage, not free
I'm trying to reach a generation with their hats turned back
Afros and cornrows sporting stocking wave caps
I'm trying to reach a generation with the colored dyed hair
Head banging to rock music with the piercings everywhere
I'm trying to reach a generation with the skull tattoos
Dressed in all black, depressed gothic-wearing crews
I'm trying to reach a generation that call themselves the "mac"
Motivated by insecurities losing their virginity, but wanting it back
I'm trying to reach a generation of those raised in foster homes
Crying at night, full of pain, abused and all alone
I'm trying to reach a generation molested and raped by those they trusted
Struggling with their identity, they look in the mirror and feel disgusted
I'm trying to reach a generation full of anger and fatherless
Seeing violent shootings and screaming mothers while

their loved ones are put to rest
I'm trying to reach a generation
Help me reach them, Lord
Help me reach them.

—Kelvin Dwan Curry

Preface

Hey, what's up? I'm glad you decided to check out what this "I'm telling the truth" business is all about. You'll be glad that you did! Now, before we get started, let me share a simple and yet familiar experience that we have all had. I'm sure that each of you has seen a movie that was a love story.

Now I know the ladies know what I'm talking about because you probably could name your favorite one right now if I asked you. And as for the guys out there, you probably watched what we call a "chick flick" only because your girlfriend or your wife made you. You know the ones where all the women "ahh" when the guy in the movie does something that is so sweet and romantic.

It's funny because my wife, Melanie, and I are huge movie lovers! And even though we love going to the movies, we also like renting movies and hanging out at the house with the popcorn on the couch as we watch it. I remember one particular time (out of the many) that she really wanted us to rent this movie that was supposed to be the love story of the year. Every time we went to the video store, she would come and pull me away from the action movie section and drag me over to the drama section to show me this movie. Finally, one day I gave in and said, "OK honey, I would love to watch this love story with you." And guess what, even though I am an action, thriller, and comedy movie kind of guy, I actually loved the story of this movie. As a matter of fact, after we watched it, I said to myself, "Man, that was the greatest love story I've ever seen."

But when I really thought about it for another second, the truth is that it really wasn't. As much as we all like a good love story, none even comes close in comparison to the true story that I am going to talk to you about. Do you want to know what that is? I'm telling the truth! The greatest love story ever told is the gospel of Jesus Christ! This story is far beyond any and all love stories every told and as you continue to read, you will definitely see why. My prayer is that after reading this book, you will allow this simple, yet powerful truth to radically change your life in the same way it has done mine!

Your Friend,
Kelvin

P.S. A true friend is someone who tells you the truth no matter what because they love and care about you.

Introduction

Why This Book?

There are two groups of people in the world. Group 1 are those who have a personal relationship with Jesus Christ and therefore, know God. And Group 2 are those who do not yet have a personal relationship with Jesus Christ and therefore, do not know God. No matter who you are, where you're from, or what "religion" you have chosen, you fall into one of these groups. Believe it or not, this book was actually written for both groups.

"OK I'm in Group 2. So what? What can I expect from this book?"

Through this book, you can expect the following:

You will read about God's love for you personally and the full truth about the plan He put into action or "in full effect" to show and prove that love.

You'll receive an explanation of who Jesus really is. Some say that He was just another prophet. Others say that He was just a great teacher. But this book will tell the truth about Jesus. It will show you that He is way more than a prophet or great teacher.

You will find out with certainty that Jesus is the only way to know God, get into heaven and therefore, have eternal life. There was a time in my life when I use to go to bed at night pondering questions about eternity. Where would I go when I died? Likewise, many of you are uncertain as to what happens next when your life here is over. My uncertainty of the answer to this question brought about a fear of death. As a result of my personal relationship with Jesus Christ, I no longer have that fear of death. Instead, I have the unbelievable joy of eternal life. I now have a certainty of where I will spend eternity. This book will offer the key to freedom from the fear of death, so that you too, might have the certainty of eternal life in Christ Jesus our Lord.

You'll have the opportunity of a lifetime to respond to

God's love for you through Jesus Christ by allowing Him to be your best friend. Many people are unsure as to what life is all about. I mean, what is the meaning of life and why are we here? What is our purpose? Many of you have tried to fill the void in your life through drugs, sex, relationships, money, success, you name it. We have all been there and it can be different for each person. These substitutes can be fun for the moment and even seem to get the "job done" for a while. But in the end, you have still found yourself feeling empty inside. The question is: What is missing in my life? What is the real permanent solution that will really meet my need for everlasting fulfillment? This book will prove how a relationship with God through His Son, Jesus Christ, is the answer to all these questions. Through this book, I will invite you to experience the awesome joy and peace that this relationship brings.

I'm a Christian. I have a personal relationship with Jesus. What can I expect from this book?

Let me start off by telling you what I have observed by working in youth ministry and with teenagers in general for several years. You have to understand that reaching youth is my calling. I mean, all you children and teens out there, ya'll are my heart. I love each and every one of you, for real! I really do! My style of ministry is just being myself and that means sharing my life and the love of Jesus with kids. After hanging out and talking to Christian youth, I realized that whether they were new believers or those who had been saved for a while, there was a common thread among many of them. Here's the scoop. Although these youth had a relationship with Jesus, they struggled with communicating their faith to others. More specifically, they were not equipped (like many adult Christians) to effectively communicate the whole truth of what they believed and why they believed it.

Often times, youth ministries encourage Christian teens to tell their friends at school and on their block about Jesus (aka evangelize). Youth evangelism is great because youth are more likely to respond to the love of Christ when it's presented by their peers. Once a person accepts Christ and God changes their life, they have a story to tell. This story is called their *testimony*. The story of one person will save another because it's like if God did it for you, I'm sure He can do it for me. This book will encourage you to be bold in sharing your testimony of how God saved you while addressing the legitimate need to be able to share the specifics of your faith in Jesus.

Through this book, you can expect to learn to effectively communicate:

What you believe (exactly in detail).

Why you believe it (the basis of your faith).

In essence, you will learn to share the gospel of Jesus Christ in its entirety. The reason that this information is important for every Christian, not just teens, is because we live in a society where there are tons of religions that deny that Jesus is the *only way* to know God. So, when they hear about Jesus, they automatically have many questions. These questions can be answered only if you have a firm foundation in what you believe and why you believe it. In other words, I can know the truth, but to reach my family, friends, peers, and just someone in general, I have to be able to present the truth in a way they can understand.

Many people live in confusion because the world offers a "variety pack" of religion. However, when the truth is communicated, it will dispel their confusion so that they can clearly see that there is only one God and that the only way to know Him is through His Son, Jesus Christ. Some will accept the truth and some will reject it. Don't sweat it. Just tell it! You see, this gospel that I preach is meant to be received and shared. It's like telling a friend about a really good movie you saw, not out of duty but because you really liked it so you can't wait to tell somebody! This is my motivation. God has saved me. Now it's like I can't help but tell somebody because it's literally a matter of life and death! My prayer is that this book will get you out of the norm and give you that sense of reality and urgency from the heart of God. It's about time to get this thing started. In short, this book has also been written for all Christians as a tool that I hope will be helpful in communicating the full message of the gospel of this new life in Jesus Christ.

> Go, stand and speak to the people in the temple the whole message of this Life (Acts 5:20).

Chapter 1

What's the Gospel?

The word *gospel* actually means "good news." If you were to ask me to please sum up the gospel of Jesus Christ in only three words, I would say: "God loves you!" That's it! The heart of the gospel is just that simple. God loves you! I know you might ask, "How do I know that He loves me?" Well, the answer to this question is that He tells us in His Word, the Bible. Let's read the following scripture together:

> For God so *loved* the world, that He gave His only begotten Son, that whoever believes in Him shall not perish, but have eternal life. For God did not send the Son into the world to judge the world, but that the world might be saved through Him.—John 3:16–17, emphasis added

Many of you have heard this scripture so many times that it really doesn't mean anything to you. Maybe you remember it from Sunday school when you were younger or maybe someone in your life, such as, your grandmother, has told you before. However, no matter if you've heard it or not, God wants to make this scripture alive to you today so that you might see what it really means. Let me break it down. Let's look at the first part of verse 16: "For God so loved *the world*" (John 3:16, emphasis added). "The world" means you, me, and everybody everywhere! God loves everybody on the face of the earth. It doesn't matter who you are.

Telling the Truth #1:
God loves everybody the same, no matter what.
God's love for us is all the same no matter our race or

nationality, culture, religion, background, or even sexual preference. However, don't misunderstand what I'm saying when I mention religion, sexual preference, and culture. I am not saying that God always agrees with the religion or sexual preference we choose. I am simply saying that His *love* for you is the same, regardless of your choice. In addition, the way of life that is accepted in one's culture in not always consistent with the lifestyle that God desires.

God loves me the same no matter my race, nationality, or place of origin.

Some people teach and believe that God loves one particular race or ethnic group more than another. Many people even think that there is a superior race or nationality that is God's favorite. This belief is simply not true at all. It makes no difference which country we are from or the color of our skin. God created each and every one of us (Ps. 100:3) and He loves all of us equally.

God loves me the same, no matter what culture I am from.

The Bible says in Acts 10:34–35 that "God is not one to show partiality, but in every nation, the person who fears [to reverence; to regard with respect or awe] Him and does what is right is welcome to Him." That means that God does not discriminate against or show preference to any specific group of people. In fact, it is clear that God will accept all those who reverence Him and offer their lives in obedience to Him—without showing any partiality on His part. Therefore, regardless of our cultural backgrounds, whether it's American, Asian, African, Spanish, or another culture, God's love for each one of us is the same. This principle of God's love also relates to subcultures. A good illustration of this includes the subcultures of music within our international youth culture. Although God may not agree with the messages of their music, God still loves the guy who likes rap music just as much as the girl who loves country music.

God loves me the same no matter what my religion is.

Let me first answer a question that many of you have asked or thought at some point in your life. Here's the question, "Does God love Christians more than He loves Muslims, Buddhists, atheists, and other people who practice different religions?" Please, listen very carefully to the answer and receive my encouragement. The answer to the question is, "No." God does not love Christians any more than He loves Muslims, Buddhists, atheists, or members of other religions. Remember the scripture says, "God so loved the world." Are there Christians in the world? Are there Muslims in the world? Are there atheists in the world? The answer to all these questions is of course, "Yes."

It is important for you to understand that there is only one God and His name is Jesus. There are two groups of people in this world, as I mentioned in my introduction. Group 1 are those who have a personal relationship with Jesus Christ and therefore, know God. And Group 2 are those who do not have a personal relationship with Jesus Christ and therefore, do not know God. No matter who you are or what religion you have chosen, you fall into one of these groups. Christianity is not just another religion. True Christianity is a relationship with God through His Son, Jesus Christ. It's all about relationship with the true and living God. The fact is that all religions that deny that Jesus is the Son of God and is the only way to receive eternal life (salvation) are false religions serving false gods. We all know that if something is false, that means it is fake or not real. God loves us all so much that He wants us to know Him for who He really is. He doesn't want us to be deceived for another minute. My definition of *deceived* is thinking you're doing the right thing but in reality you're doing the wrong thing. God's love desires to bring us out of the lies and deception of false religions and into a right relationship with Him. When somebody loves you, I mean truly loves you, they want you to know the truth. Jesus is the truth.

God loves me the same
no matter what my background is.

Some of you hear the truth about God's love for you and find it hard to believe because of your background. You hear that God loves you, but it doesn't penetrate your heart as truth because you feel unworthy to receive this love. For example, a lot of you have been abused sexually, physically, emotionally, or verbally. As a result, you have asked the question, "If God loves me so much, then why did these horrible things happen to me?" Many of you have felt that maybe God is punishing you or that there is something wrong with you. You've thought to yourself, "I must be bad," or "What did I do wrong to deserve this?" The truth is that God created each person with a free will that enables them to make their own decisions. Therefore, the people or person who hurt you made some bad decisions that affected you. That means that you didn't do anything wrong. It wasn't your fault and God was not punishing you. God loves you too much to ever hurt you and He never wanted those bad things to happen. In fact, His love for you is so strong that He wants to heal you of those emotional scars and wounds that the abuse has caused.

You might say, "That sounds good, but I'm in prison. Does God still love me, too?" Let me shoot this to you as straight as I can. Remember I said that God loves you no matter what? No matter what means no matter what. No matter what you've done or how many mistakes you've made, God still loves you! I don't care if you are a prostitute or a choirgirl; it makes no difference. It doesn't matter if you were raised in a bad neighborhood or a good neighborhood. Whatever your background, God loves you exactly the same! Please hear that truth and receive it. "God so loved the world"—that world includes you!

God loves me the same
no matter what my sexual preference is.

There has been much discussion about sexual preference

and how it relates to one's relationship with God and His love. I want to clear some things up for my dear friends who struggle with their sexuality and engage in homosexual or lesbian relationships. I first want you to know that no matter what you have heard, God loves you the same as He does the heterosexual person. There is no difference in that love. Secondly, God isn't mad at you. Thirdly, although God loves you, He does not agree with your lifestyle because He created man and woman to be together, not man and man, or woman and woman. God's love wants the best for you and that's why He desires to bring you out of the homosexual or lesbian lifestyle and into a right relationship with Him. He wants to help you realize your true identity by being who He created you to be. I apologize for the mixed messages that the church has given by condoning gay bishops and other gay or lesbian clergy members. This occurrence is not OK. Know that God is clear on His position about this subject. Homosexuality is sin (to disobey God) and His love has made a way for all of us to be free from whatever sin we may struggle with. Sin is sin, whether it's homosexuality, anger, adultery, gossip, or whatever else. Sin is always displeasing in the eyes of God. God desires to set us free from sin and the destructive nature that it has on our lives. Let's pray:

> *Lord Jesus, I pray that you would touch the heart of each person reading this who is struggling with their sexuality and identity. I pray that You would invade their souls with the power of Your love and heal them of every emotional scar that has been plaguing them for so long. Jesus, open their hearts to receive You right now and set them completely free from the lifestyle of homosexuality. I pray that You would cause them to realize their true identity in You, Christ, as the person You created them to be. Amen.*

Allow me to now draw your attention back to the text in John 3:16. The first part of this scripture reads:
For God so loved the world. —John 3:16

I want you to take a look at the word "so" in that verse (see above). We often read the verse kind of dry. However, we should read it with passion and emphasis on the word *so* in order to bring out the heart and emotion of what God is really communicating:

> For God so loved the world that He gave His only begotten Son that whoever believes in Him shall not perish, but have eternal life. —John 3:16, emphasis added

Let me explain so you can understand this. I want all of you teenagers to think of the times when you go out to the mall with your friends. A lot of you girls pretend like you are always going to buy something or window shop, but you know goodness well that most of the time it's so you can look at guys. And guys, you know when you are there with your friends you're checking out the ladies. I know what's up! Now ladies, when you see a really cute guy, you say, "Girl, that guy is *so* cute!" Or guys when you see a girl that you really like, you might say, "Dude, look. Man, that girl is *so* fine!" Here's the point. The word *so* emphasizes how good someone looks. When you say, "So good," you are emphasizing the level of good you are trying to communicate. It's different than if you just would have said that the person looks good. The "so good," means more than just "good" because it puts the good in a higher category.

When we read John 3:16 that "God *so loved* the world," the word *so* is emphasizing how much God loves us. God doesn't just love us. No, God loves us a lot. It's saying that His love for us isn't average; it's a great and awesome love!

> For God so *loved* the world that He *gave* His only begotten Son that whoever believes in Him shall not perish, but have eternal life. —John 3:16, emphasis added

Now that we know that God's love for us is emphasized as being great and awesome and not average, we can't just stop there. We have to take it a step further by answering a very important question. Here's the question: "What *kind of love* does God have for us?"

Now, we know that this love is way beyond average. However, we still need to understand what this kind of love is like. We need to know what the scripture means when we see "loved" mentioned in the first part of verse 16. For example, does this love mean the same thing as when we say: "I love pizza, I love going to the mall, I love watching television, or I love my boyfriend?" Is this the kind of love that God has for you? Or does His love for you present a much deeper meaning? You see, it's not just good enough to know in my mind that someone loves me, but I need to know the manner or the type of that love. "What does this love look like?" "Does this love look like any love that I have ever seen or known?" These are the questions we need to answer.

Telling the Truth #2: The kind of love that God has for us is the kind of love that would give up your life to be killed for someone who doesn't even know you.

Jesus died for you!

The Bible says, "He gave … " You see God's love is a love beyond words. I like to refer to it as a "love in action." It is a passionate love. God didn't just tell us that He loved us and that was it, end of story. Nope. He proved His love by actually doing something to express it to us. I guess you could say that God didn't just talk the talk, but He walked the walk! As a married man, I can tell my wife, Melanie, that I love her every day all day long if I wanted to. However, if I never did anything to show her that what I was saying with my mouth I meant with my heart, it wouldn't really mean anything. My "I love you" would just be empty words.

God didn't just give us lip service. He is a "show and prove" type of God. He demonstrated His love for us 2,000 years ago, by sending His One and Only Son, Jesus, to earth to die on a cross by *crucifixion* for our sins. Jesus never committed any sins, but He knew that all of us had or would commit sins. Since sin is punished by death (as you will learn in Chapter 2), Jesus wanted to spare us from dying a death because of sin. So He took our place on the cross even though He knew some of us would not receive Him or believe the fact that He died for us. Still, the only way to be saved from this death is to receive Him and what He did on the cross for all of us.

What is a crucifixion? And what actually happened to a person being crucified?

Crucifixion was common in Bible days. It was the most painful and humiliating practice that the Romans used to execute their hardened criminals. The punishment of the crucifixion process was extremely excruciating because the criminals were first scourged, the act of being beaten severely with a whip that had pieces of metal or bones attached to the ends. The scourging was so severe that many people didn't even survive that. One of the purposes of scourging was to basically get you to the point where you were so close to dying that when you were actually crucified, your death could be expedited. After the scourging, the person was made to carry their crossbeam (tied to their body) to the execution site. When they reached the execution site, which was generally a public place, they were then nailed to a cross (crossbeam attached to an upright wooden stake or pole) and left to die publicly. Jesus proved His love for us by dying in this way even though He was completely innocent and without sin.

God made Him who had no sin to be sin for us, so that in him we might become the righteousness of God. — 2 Corinthians 5:21, niv

They took Jesus, therefore, and He went out, bearing

His own cross, to the place called the Place of a Skull, which is called in Hebrew, Golgotha. There they crucified Him, and with Him two other men, one on either side, and Jesus in between –John 19:17–18

It was now about the sixth hour, and darkness fell over the whole land until the ninth hour, because the sun was obscured; and the veil of the temple was torn in two. And Jesus, crying out with a loud voice, said, "Father, INTO YOUR HANDS I COMMIT MY SPIRIT." Having said this, He breathed His last. Now when the centurion [an officer in the Roman army in charge of 100 soldiers] saw what had happened, he began praising God, saying, 'Certainly this man was innocent.' And all the crowds who came together for this spectacle, when they observed what had happened, began to return, beating their breasts. —Luke 23:44–48

Can you imagine going through hours of torture being whipped so badly with whips that had pieces of metal or bone attached to the ends that it literally ripped and pulled chunks of your flesh right off your body? Or how about gasping for air in total agony as you keep slipping in a pool of your own blood? Then think about having a crown of thorns being pressed so deeply into your head that blood gushes down your entire face? And if that wasn't enough, then think about deciding to go through with offering up your own body to be nailed (in both wrists and feet) to a cross (seven to nine feet high) with no anesthesia and going through hours of agonizing pain and suffering until death for someone that doesn't even know you? This is the kind of sacrificial love that God has for us! It is literally out of this world and beyond me! I encourage you to just take a moment to think about this kind of love and then check out what the Bible says in the book of Romans:

You see, at just the right time, when we were still

powerless, Christ died for the ungodly. Very rarely will anyone die for a righteous man, though for a good man someone might possibly dare to die. But God demonstrates His own love for us in this: While we were still sinners, Christ died for us. Since we have now been justified by his blood, how much more shall we be saved from God's wrath through Him! For if, when we were God's enemies, we were reconciled to Him through the death of His Son, how much more, having been reconciled, shall we be saved through his life! —Romans 5:6–10, niv

How many of you are soldiers or know someone who is a soldier? Let's take for example a husband who goes off to war leaving behind his wife and five children for the cause of freedom. This soldier is willing to die in battle, if necessary, so that his family can enjoy a life of liberty. This liberty is what he is fighting so hard for. It's a kind of love that's sacrificial in nature. The love of the soldier is great, patriotic and worthy of being commended. The kind of love that Jesus has for you is similar but on a whole other level.

You see the soldier is willing to die for the love of his family and country. His family includes people that know him, love him and support him. His country includes people that may not know him personally, but support him and love what he is doing. In comparison, God's love for us through His Son, Jesus Christ, is a kind of love that was willing to die for His very enemies! If any soldier said that they were leaving their family and all of their love ones to go die a for sure death for their enemies, you would think he or she was crazy. Well guess what? God stepped down from heaven and entered humanity as Jesus, the God man (100 percent God and 100 percent man) to do just that—die for His enemies!

Notice what Romans 5:8 says, "But God demonstrates his own love for us in this: While we were still sinners, Christ died for us" (niv). This scripture means that when we didn't even know God (in our sin state of being), we were considered enemies of God (Rom. 5:10). Yet, He loved us so much that He sent Jesus to die for us anyway. Wow! Is there any greater love than that? Also notice that is says, "His own love for us." Who is the "us" in this sentence? The "us" is you and me. And "His own love" makes it personal. God's love is not a hand-me-down love! God's love for you is His own. He loves you specifically and personally. You, yes you, matter to God! And you don't just matter to Him end of story, but you matter to Him a lot and in a very, very personal "just between Me and you" kind of way. It's like God has a special framed picture of you on His desk in heaven that He looks at every day saying, "I love her so much! I love him so much! Say this with me, "God loves me, [say your name]. Yes, me, [say your name]!" In the Greek, the original language of the New Testament, this love is actually referred to as agape, the highest level of love that exists. It is totally unconditional, unwaveringly sacrificial and focused solely on serving the interest of others, no matter the cost. This love is the kind of love that motivated Jesus to pay the price for you and me with His very life.

Jesus was resurrected (raised from the dead) just for you!

Thank God that it doesn't just end with Jesus's death. The Bible says that He was resurrected (raised from the dead) by the power of God on the third day.

> On the first day of the week, very early in the morning, the women took the spices they had prepared and went to the tomb. They found the stone rolled away from the tomb, but when they entered, they did not find the body of the Lord Jesus. While they were wondering about this, suddenly two men in clothes that gleamed like lightning stood beside them. In their fright the women bowed down with their faces to the ground, but the men said to them, "Why do you look for the living among the dead? He is not here; he has risen!

Remember how he told you, while he was still with you in Galilee: 'The Son of Man must be delivered into the hands of sinful men, be crucified and on the third day be raised again.'" —Luke 24:1–7, niv

Now there is another part of this event that is important for you to understand. Here's the deal. Although many people debate the question, Who killed Jesus? It is basically null and void because Jesus *gave up* His own life, by His own choice. He had the power and authority to lay it down and raise it back up again:

The thief [the devil] comes only to steal and kill and destroy; I came that they may have life, and have it more abundantly. I am the good shepherd; the good shepherd lays down His life for the sheep. —John 10:10–11

The reason my Father loves me is that I lay down my life—only to take it up again. No one takes it from me, but I lay it down of my own accord. I have authority to lay it down and authority to take it up again. This command I received from my Father. —John 10:17–18, niv

The whole purpose of Jesus being resurrected from the dead was so that those who believe in Him would also be resurrected from the dead when they die:

Jesus said to her, "I am the resurrection and the life. He who believes in me will live, even though he dies; and whoever lives and believes in me will never die." —John 11:25–26, niv

God promises us life after death if we believe in Him. Therefore, Jesus, by His resurrection, straight up "body slammed" the *fear of death* and put it out for the count for good.

Maybe you are like I used to be and you go to sleep at night and have that thought of, "Where would I go if I died?" I had a fear of death because I wasn't sure about how to answer that question. I just wasn't positive about life after death and that scared me. I know there are so many of you who know exactly what I'm talking about because that's where you are today. I want you to know that you can have the same assurance and confidence that I now have concerning life after death. Jesus conquered death through His crucifixion and resurrection so you could enjoy life and sleep in peace without worry or fear. He basically "got your back" on the matter long before you were ever born!

> Since the children have flesh and blood, he too shared in their humanity so that by his death he might destroy him who holds the power of death—that is, the devil— and free those who all their lives were held in slavery by their fear of death. —Hebrews 2:14–15, niv

Jesus's resurrection has changed everything for you and me because it is living proof of life after death for those who accept Him. You see, this is the promise for those who put their faith in Jesus. The promise is that the same power that raised Jesus from the dead will also raise you up when you die to be with Him. Jesus was also resurrected so that we too could be resurrected into what the Bible calls the "newness" of life or a new life right here on Earth:

> We were therefore buried with him through baptism into death in order that, just as Christ was raised from the dead through the glory of the Father, we too may live a new life. —Romans 6:4, niv

In other words, when Jesus comes into my life, His resurrection power then lives on the inside of me. This power can change my life and make me a new person. You see, many of you out there are acting like someone you're not, often because we feel insecure about ourselves and we want to fit in with the crowd (whoever the crowd is). Please don't feel bad because it's not your fault that you feel insecure. You didn't wake up this morning and say, "Yes I will have jelly on my toast, a big bowl of cereal and side of insecurity please!" No! I'm sure you didn't wake up saying that, right? The reason you feel insecure is simply because you don't know who you are. Why is that? It's because you can never truly know who you are as a person apart from Christ. The real you, your true identity is rooted in Jesus Christ because He is God and He created you. You are a masterpiece created by a great artist. Getting to know Him will help you to see what He had in mind when He created you. So He has to come into your life so that He might live His life through you, and therefore you become yourself, your true self. When Jesus lives through you, He will open the gifts and abilities that He placed in you and lead you to accomplish what He planned for you to do on Earth.

When Jesus comes onto the scene of our life, His resurrection power in us by His Holy Spirit (God's Spirit in you) can make us new as though we were born all over again. To be real about it, that's exactly what happens. You become born again! It doesn't matter what your age is, you could be eight, sixteen, thirty-five, or sixty-five. The moment you receive Jesus and His Holy Spirit comes and lives on the inside of you, you are born again. The only thing is that this time, you become the person God always created you to be. This is why Jesus said, "I tell you the truth, no one can enter the kingdom of God unless he is born of water and the Spirit" (John 3:5, niv).

Break It Down!

For God so loved the world, that He gave His only begotten Son, *that whoever believes in Him shall not perish*, but have eternal life. —John 3:16, emphasis added

Now that we know the manner in which God so greatly loves us and what He did to prove it, let's check out what's next. The next part of John 3:16 says, "that whoever believes in Him shall not perish." Look at the word *believes*. This word simply means to place your trust or faith in something or someone. Therefore, when I believe in Jesus, I put my faith in Him by accepting Him as the only Truth. Now, let's check out the word "perish."

What does it mean to perish?

The word *perish* means to destroy. In this verse it is referring to "eternal destruction" or "eternal death." Eternal death is to be in total separation from God forever in the ultimate and constant torment of hell (lake of fire). Hell is not just a made-up, scary movie; it is a real place that is worse than any horror flick could ever portray as this verse in Revelation reveals: "And I saw the dead, great and small, standing before the throne, and books were opened. Another book was opened, which is the book of life. The dead were judged according to what they had done as recorded in the books. If anyone's name was not found written in the book of life, he was thrown into the lake of fire" (Rev. 20:12, 15, niv).

There will be many people who will be sentenced to this terrible place on the Day of Judgment as this verse in Revelation is talking about. That's why my whole purpose for writing this book is so that you won't be in that number! I want your name to be written in the Book of Life. After you breathe your last breath and die (physically), the real you lives on. The real you is your spirit and your sprit lives forever because it's eternal. This concept is what I call "The lights being turned off, but the party's not over!" Hell was never created for any human being to experience but was a place of torment prepared by God for Satan (aka Lucifer or the devil) and the other angles who disobeyed God (Matt. 25:41). John 3:16 tells us that those who believe in Jesus (accept Him as the truth) will not go to hell (perish) but have eternal life.

Break It Down!

For God so loved the world, that He gave His only begotten Son, that whoever believes in Him shall not perish, but have *eternal life*. —John 3:16, emphasis added

What is eternal life?

John 3:16 says that "whoever believes in Him shall not perish, but have eternal life." This is what I call the invitation given to us by God to respond to His awesome love. I love it because the invitation is free and there are no strings attached! Eternal life is relationship with God through His Son, Jesus Christ, that results in spending forever and ever (eternity) with Him. Check out what Jesus prayed in the Book of John:

> After Jesus said this, he looked toward heaven and prayed: "Father, the time has come. Glorify your Son, that your Son may glorify you. For you granted him authority over all people that he might give eternal life to all those you have given him. Now this is eternal life: that they may know you, the only true God, and Jesus Christ, whom you have sent." —John 17:1–3, niv

Eternal life begins the moment I receive Jesus. Living forever and never separated from God is a result that comes with knowing Him. It's all a part of the package! It's like going to a fast-food place and ordering the value meal. Well, you get your burger (or chicken sandwich in my case), but it comes with fries and a drink, as well. It's all a part of the value meal. The same is true with eternal life. When you "order" eternal life, you accept Jesus in relationship and living forever with Him comes with it. In other words, if you've got Jesus, you've got eternal life. Therefore, when you die, you will get to go to heaven where you will experience the most ultimate joy and happiness beyond your greatest imagination! There is no sickness, disease, fear, or any other type of physical or emotional pain. It is a place where Jesus wipes every tear from your eyes and much, much more! This scripture in Revelation gives us just a small glimpse of what it will be like: "Never again will they hunger; never again will they thirst. The sun will not beat upon them, nor any scorching heat. For the Lamb [Jesus] at the center of the throne will be their shepherd; he will lead them to springs of living water. And God will wipe away every tear from their eyes" (Rev. 7:16–17, NIV).

It is also important to add that eternal life with Jesus does not just include the duration of life—the forever and ever part, never separate from Him. In fact, eternal life with Jesus also includes the quality of life. That's why Jesus said, "I came that they may have life, and have it abundantly" (John 10:10). This means that eternal life with Jesus includes an excellent quality of life that delivers true fulfillment and that lasts forever. In short, eternal life in its entirety can be described as an awesome, "off the hook," forever and ever relationship with Jesus that is kicked off the second I accept Him. Your forever and ever with God can start today!

What if I'm a good person, will that get me into heaven to have eternal life?

Notice what God *does not* say in John 3:16. He does not say if:

"I'm a good person I will have eternal life."

"I do a lot of good works, I will have eternal life."

"I just go to church, I will have eternal life."

"My parents or other family members are Christians I will have eternal life."

"I know God exists and He's real, I will have eternal life."

"I talk to God all the time, I will have eternal life."

"I believe in a god that I want to believe in whether its Allah, Buddha or whatever other religion I decide, I will have eternal life."

For a long time before I came to Christ, I thought that I was OK with God because I considered myself to be a good person. I guess you could say that I had the "good person" religion. I felt that since I wasn't a bad person and I didn't do really bad things like a lot of other people in this world, I was cool. I used to think that when it was my time to face God, I would have a really good chance of getting into heaven. I never thought that someone like me, being good and all, could ever wind up in hell. Like many of you, I thought that hell was really only for the hard-core criminals who did really "bad things" in life like murder and rape. Man, was I deceived! Jesus said, "No one is good except God alone" (Luke 18:19). Therefore, no matter how much of a good person I think I am, that will not give me eternal life.

What if I do a lot of good works, will that get me into heaven to have eternal life?

A lot of people believe that if they just perform good works and do good things for others, they will reserve their spot in heaven. Good works means doing stuff like feeding the poor, giving money to charities, taking care of the senior citizens, walking your grandmother across the street, and the list goes on and on. Now, don't misunderstand me. These are all good things to do and there is nothing wrong with doing them. God is very pleased when we serve other people. However, when you think that you can earn your salvation by doing all of these works, you are deceived. There is nothing we can do to earn our way into heaven, no matter what many religions may teach. In fact, when we're not in right relationship with God and we try to come to Him based on our righteous acts, then even these right things we are doing will be like filthy rags in His sight (Isa. 64:6). So here's the deal. I can do all the "rights things" in life and still end up having a one-way ticket to hell.

If I just go to church, will that get me into heaven to have eternal life?

I've noticed that when I've talk to a lot people about God, a few have responded by saying, "Well, I go to church regularly and I very seldom miss!" Going to church is great and it is important to go to a good Christ-centered, Bible-believing church so that you can grow in your relationship with God. However, if you don't have a relationship with God, then just going to church for "church sake" is not effective, nor will it get you into heaven. I know you have probably heard this before but going to church does not make you a Christian having eternal life anymore than sleeping in your garage makes you a car.

If my parents or family members are Christians, will that get me into heaven to have eternal life?

Almost every family, if not all families, have some members of the family that know God and some who don't. You might be a teenager of Christian parents and although you're not feeling the whole "Jesus thing" yet, they still love you enough to make sure you go to church with them. However, like everyone else, you have to come to know God for yourself. Maybe others of you have a grandmother who is the "spiritual backbone" of the family and she is always talking to you about God and praying for everybody. Well, no matter which family members represent that godly influence, my heart goes out to you! Maybe this book can be that added piece of encouragement to help you make the decision to have a personal relationship with Jesus. I pray that you do it today because you won't be able to get into heaven on the coattails of anyone else.

Believe me when I tell you that there is no better time to accept God in your life than right now! Being a Christian is not boring. God wants to have a unique relationship with you that is going to be different than your entire family's relationship with God. You don't have to worry about being like somebody else. God will show you who you are in Christ as the person He created you to be. Why? Because Jesus loves you and wants to be your best friend. Today is the day of salvation for you! Take a hold of it before it's too late! I really care about you.

Please don't let this moment pass you by. God wanted me to write this book, just for you. I dedicate this scripture to you: "For He says, 'In the time of my favor I heard you, and in the day of salvation I helped you.' I tell you, now is the time of God's favor, now is the day of salvation" (2 Cor. 6:2, niv).

If I know that God exists and that He's real, won't this in itself get me into heaven to have eternal life?

If we would all admit it, we all know that God exists. We are really without excuse. All we have to do to know that there is a God is go outside and look at the blue sky, the trees, the birds in the air, stars in the sky, the mountains and all other creation.

> For since the creation of the world His invisible attributes, His eternal power and divine nature, have been clearly seen, being understood through what has been made, so that they are without excuse. —Romans 1:20

We even know by considering the intricate makeup of the human being that there is a greater power who created us and everything else. However, here's the kicker. Knowing that there is a God and knowing God are two totally different things! The Bible says that faith without works is dead (James 2:17). In other words, I can believe that God exists and that He loves me, but I might not believe in Him enough to do something in response to that love. As a result, my knowledge of God and His existence becomes useless.

> You believe that God is one. You do well; the demons also believe, and shudder. But are you willing to recognize, you foolish fellow, that faith without works is useless? —James 2:19–20

If I talk to God all the time, won't that get me into heaven to have eternal life?

I have to tell you that this idea is one of the biggest misconceptions when it comes to truly knowing God. Trust me when I tell you that God does know your heart even when others may judge you and He loves it when you talk to Him. Many of you are in a place where God is working on you and even though you haven't committed your life to Him in relationship yet, you do recognize your need for Him. However, here's the tricky part. Some of you have been living this way of just "dating" God for so long that it has become a lifestyle of what you now believe makes you and Him "cool." Now, He is always "cool" with you because He loves you. However, you are not cool with Him from your side of the relationship because you have not committed yourself to Him. I used the phrase "dating God" for a very distinct reason. Why? Because when you're dating somebody, you are essentially open to seeing other people if someone else comes along that you think is better than your current partner. I know that many of you date several people at a time just for that fact. The point is that the dating game stops when you decide to make the commitment and get married. Here's what's up. God wants to "marry" you. This means that He wants you to fully commit your life to Him. Yes, put it into His hands. You can trust Him. I want to tell you that no matter what you think, it's not too late for you. You can commit your life to Him this very minute. He's right there with you, knocking at the door of your heart!

> Behold, I stand at the door and knock; if anyone hears My voice and opens the door, I will come in to him and will dine with him, and he with Me. —Revelation 3:20

God wants your whole heart. Can you see that? He's after your heart. Don't bother trying to clean yourself up before you come to Him. He loves you and wants you just the way you are! I don't know who you are, but God is speaking to you and you can feel it! It's OK. Let Him in.

Will I still get into heaven and have eternal life as long as I believe in a god that I want to believe in whether it's Allah, Buddha or whatever religion I decide?

What I am about to say is very important. The biggest deception in our world today is that there are several ways to get to the same God. Wrong! Wrong! Wrong! This belief is what I call the "all inclusive" religion. I know it may sound like it makes sense to you, but please know that it's simply not true. It's hard not to think its OK because it's being promoted everywhere. I mean just yesterday while Melanie and I were driving down a main highway here in our city, we saw a big billboard that read, "Different Faiths, Same God" being advertised by a certain religious organization. What makes it so deceptive is that this whole idea promotes "unity." So when you hear "unity" and bringing people of all faiths together, it obviously sounds like the right thing to do. God doesn't blame you or these organizations for believing this way because you just don't know the truth until someone tells you. That's what deception is all about. Remember my definition of *deceived*: "thinking you're doing the right thing but in reality you're doing the wrong thing." God doesn't fault you for that. He loves you and wants to expose the lie by revealing the truth to you. Jesus is the truth and the only way to God the Father is through Him.

> Jesus said to him, "I am the way, and the truth, and the life; no one comes to the Father but through Me."
> —John 14:6

When Jesus says, "the life," He is referring to "eternal life." Therefore, eternal life is in Jesus alone, not another religion.

Furthermore, when its comes to unity among the religious communities of different beliefs, please be advised as to what Jesus said:

> Therefore everyone who confesses Me before men, I will also confess him before My Father who is in heaven. But whoever denies Me before men, I will also deny him before My Father who is in heaven. Do not think that I came to bring peace on the earth; I did not come to bring peace, but a sword. For I came to SET A MAN AGAINST HIS FATHER, AND A DAUGHTER AGAINST HER MOTHER, AND A DAUGHER-IN-LAW AGAINST HER MOHTER-IN-LAW; and A MAN'S ENEMIES WILL BE THE MEMBERS OF HIS HOUSEHOLD. He who loves father or mother more than Me is not worthy of Me; and he who loves son or daughter more than Me is not worthy of Me. And he who does not take his cross and follow after Me is not worthy of Me. He who has found his life will lose it, and he who has lost his life for My sake will find it. —Matthew 10:32–39

Jesus said that He did not come to bring peace but a *sword*. What does a sword do? A sword cuts. It divides. In other words, Jesus didn't come to bring everybody together. He came as the dividing truth. I call this the "Jesus Factor." What will you do with Jesus? You see, there are really only two groups of people: those who accept Jesus Christ and those that reject Him. In our religious community we have those who believe the truth about Jesus's divinity and others who write Him off as just another great prophet or teacher who eventually died. However, Jesus is not dead, He was raised from the dead by His own power and is alive today! In addition, these two groups exist among our own families. That's what Jesus meant when He said He came to set family members against one another (Matt. 10:35).

Telling the Truth #3: You can't get into heaven on your own terms,you have to do it God's way.

Think about it.

Here's the deal. God's invitation to us is to have eternal life with Him by believing on the Lord Jesus Christ and therefore escaping the torment of hell. The questions you have to ask yourself are, "Where do I want to go when I die?" "Where do I want to spend eternity?" "On that Day of Judgment when I stand before God, will I be confident and excited, knowing that I have everlasting life waiting for me? Or will I be scared and fearful knowing that I had my chances, but I rejected God's love and refused to accept the truth?"

Break It Down!

For God *did not send* the Son into the world to *judge the world*, but that the world might be saved through Him. —John 3:17, emphasis added

I want you to catch this with all of your heart. Many people think that God is a forever, angry God who is just waiting for us to mess up so He can push this big red button from His "heavenly command center" and send us to hell. No! That is not who God is at all. This is who God is:

The LORD is compassionate and gracious, Slow to anger and abounding in lovingkindness. —Psalm 103:8

Regardless of what you've heard or thought, God is not mad at you. Let me say it again because it is one of the biggest misconceptions about God. God is not angry or mad at you and never will be angry or mad at you! There is a difference between someone being mad at you and being displeased with something that you are doing. God loves us even though He does not always agree with what we are doing. Our actions don't stop His love. Sometimes, when Melanie used to read the Old Testament and see God wiping out nations with fire and brimstone, she thought He'd be mad at her, too. She, like many of you, was not thinking of the fact that all of this wiping out of nations with wars, fire and floods happened before Jesus came. In fact, God realized that we couldn't get this thing called life right without His help. He didn't want to keep wiping people off. Enter the New Testament when Jesus comes to help us.

When I think of God, I see someone who is upset with me when I blow it. Why is it so hard for me to accept the fact that God is not mad at me?

Many of you have had this false view of God as being angry because people in your life have portrayed Him as having that disposition toward you. They were wrong! No matter how many times you've messed up or what you've done, God's love remains the same, overwhelmingly unconditional.

Maybe you were mistreated by an authority figure in your life (for example, parents). When you hear that God is "our Father" it can be hard to receive His love because you immediately think about the broken relationship you have with your dad. Similarly, when you are raised with parents who are always mad and get angry with you about every little mistake you make, it adds fuel to the fire of your "God view." In cases like these, you automatically grow up thinking that God is always upset with you because that's how your parents treated you all the time.

In the same way, there is another class of you who were raised in a Christian home that misrepresented God's character. Don't get me wrong. There is no perfect family no matter who you are. However, there were some lines crossed that have affected your view of who God really is. These are the homes where you make a mistake and then you're constantly reminded that there is something wrong with you. The message you get is that you better act better for God to love you and not be mad at you anymore. The rules and regulations are excessive and you're experiencing a lot of verbal and emotional abuse. The whole mind-set in this home is, "When you do good, God is pleased and when you do bad God is mad."

It's like I can see you right now as I'm writing this. I mean, as soon as you became 18, you moved out of the house and stopped going to church because you didn't "have to" anymore. You don't want God in you life and growing up you even said to yourself: "If this is what God is like, I don't want to have any part of Him." When your name comes up in a family conversation, they immediately judge you and always say that they don't know what's going on with you!

John 3:17 tells us right away that God did not send Jesus to us to judge us. The word *judge* means to condemn. It's like somebody rubbing in your face all of the terrible mistakes you've made and telling you how bad you are. God didn't send Jesus to the world to do that. God's whole reason for sending His Son Jesus is so that we might be saved through Him. Why? He loves you!

Let me encourage you. Stop blaming your parents and forgive them for acting religious. Christians can and will misrepresent God because we are all human and we get it wrong a lot. That's why it is so important to get to know God for yourself. He wants you to accept the correct view of Him as it's clearly described in the Bible (Ps.103:8). God's love for you isn't based on your performance. No, God's love for you is unconditional and that means He loves you regardless of what you do or don't do. I know it's been hard, but I pray that you would accept the true nature of God's character so that you might receive the fullness of His love for you. This is your time; let Him heal you. Every time it's hard to see Him that way, I encourage you to read Psalm 103:8 and tell yourself, "God loves me no matter what," until it becomes your "God view" reality.

Lord, I pray that you would heal all those who are reading this from their past experiences and allow them to literally feel Your unconditional love and acceptance for them in this very moment. Make it real in their hearts, so that they can experience and see You for who You really are. Amen.

Chapter 2

Why Do I Need Jesus to Be Saved?

For God did not send the Son into the world to judge the world, but that the world might be *saved* through Him." —John 3:17, emphasis added

Many of you have probably heard the word "saved" in a Christian context but you never really knew what it truly meant. Maybe you heard, "You need to be saved" or "You need to get saved." The question is, "Saved from what?"

What am I being saved from?

For all have sinned and fall short of the glory of God. —Romans 3:23

The answer is saved from the penalty of sin. What is sin? *Sin* simply means to disobey God, to miss the mark. Romans 3:23 tells us that we all sin, or disobey God. You may say, "Wait a minute. I'm a good person. I pretty much obey God and do everything the Bible says that I should." Hear this, my friends, because it's very important. It doesn't matter how much of a saint or good person you believe yourself to be. God says that there is not one human being who is without sin. Therefore, no matter who you are, you have sinned and will sin just like everybody else. It's just a fact. We all do it!

How do I know I'm a sinner?
Let's break this down a little bit further. Remember that

sin means to disobey God or miss the mark. Here's what I mean. It's the failure to achieve the standard that God has set for me to live by. What is this standard? This standard is the Bible. For example, let's examine the Ten Commandments (aka the Law), which is written in a small portion of the Old Testament.

We'll look at a few commandments and see how well we've faired so far in life.

Commandment 8: "You shall not steal" (Exod. 20:15).

Commandment 9: "You shall not bear false witness [lie] against your neighbor" (Exod. 20:16).

Have you every taken something that wasn't yours? It could have even been as small and insignificant as a paper clip. What about lying? Have you every lied about somebody else or told a little white lie to keep from getting into trouble? Well, I don't know how you're doing so far, but I'm batting a big fat zero because I've done both.

OK, let's look at a couple more commandments to see if we can improve our odds.

Commandment 3: "You shall not take the name of the LORD your God in vain" (Exod. 20:7, niv).

How about these?

Commandment 6: "You shall not murder" (Exod. 20:13).

Commandment 7: "You shall not commit adultery" (Exod. 20:14).

Now before you answer, we better read what Jesus said about these commandments: "You have heard that it was said to the people long ago, 'Do not murder, and anyone who murders will be subject to judgment.' But I tell you that anyone who is angry with his brother will be subject to judgment" (Matt. 5:21–22, NIV).

Have you ever been angry with someone? Have you every held a grudge against somebody for what they did? If the answer is "Yes," then according to Jesus, you have committed murder.

The same principle applies to adultery. In Matthew 5:27–28

Jesus says, "You have heard that it was said, 'Do not commit adultery. But I tell you that anyone who looks at a woman lustfully has already committed adultery with her in his heart" (niv).

All you married guys out there, I want you to be real now. Have you every checked out another woman, looking her up and down with lustful thoughts? And ladies, I want you to be real, too. Have you ever starred at a cute guy with lustful ideas flowing through your head even though you already had a man at home? If so, then guess what? According to God, you have committed adultery.

Now don't get me wrong, *murder* still means to *actually* kill someone. And adultery still means to *physically* sleep with someone else's wife or husband or messing around outside of your marriage. But Jesus clearly points out that it means much more than just that. I don't know about you, but it seems too easy to blow it now because of its deeper meaning. It's like now all I have to do is entertain thoughts of hatred and lust and it becomes the same as me actually doing it! Jesus said that we have committed the sin in our hearts.

Why do I sin?

We all commit sins because it's in our nature. Each and every one of us was born into sin or what is referred to as a sinful nature. That means that when you were born, you already had in you the instinct to sin. Compare it to a baby crying when he is born. Does anyone have to tell the baby to cry? Do babies have to take a class on how to cry? The answer is obviously, "No." No one tells the baby to cry, and even if they did that baby wouldn't understand them anyway. The baby just naturally cries out of instinct. Likewise, sin is just naturally committed out of a natural-born instinct.

How was I born into a sinful nature?

The reason you and I were born into a sinful nature is all because of what the Bible refers to in the Book of Genesis as the "fall of man." This is when the first human beings ever created, Adam and Eve, sinned against God by doing what Satan told them to do instead of obeying God (Gen. 3). This is how the curse of sin entered the world. From that point on, every human being born after Adam and Eve was by default born into sin.

OK, so we all sin. What's the problem? What's the big deal?

> For the *wages* of sin is death, but the free gift of God is eternal life in Christ Jesus our Lord. —Romans 6:23

Here's the problem. The wages or what I call the "payment" for a lifestyle of sin is eternal death. Think about the word *wages*. I'm sure many of you have a job, had a job, or maybe have done some type of work to earn money. *Money* is another word for *wages*. Let's say, for example, that you get paid biweekly for your job. At the end of your hard-earned two weeks, you are expecting a paycheck. Your paycheck is a *payment* for the work you did. So guess what? Romans 6:23 is literally telling us that our *payment*, what we have earned or deserve, for living a life of sin is eternal death! It hurts just to say it because we talked about eternal death in Chapter 1. Who wants to experience that? Not me, and I know you don't! Therefore, if I put two and two together I realize that I was born into sin, so I'm a sinner automatically. On top of that, payment for my sin is eternal death. Then that means I will go to hell, no questions asked, unless someone saves me!

That is why we need to be saved. Jesus is the Savior who came to save us. The good news is that we don't have to pay the penalty for our sin because Jesus paid the price for us! God never leaves us hanging. We can be saved and receive the free gift of *salvation*. *Salvation* as defined in the *Holman Bible Dictionary* is "deliverance from the guilt and power of sin." Look at the remainder of Romans 6:23, "but the free gift of

God is eternal life in Christ Jesus our Lord." Free means free. I don't have to earn it through good works and I don't loose it by making a mess of my life. Why? Because it's a free gift from God to me no matter who I am or what I've done.

Telling the Truth #4: Jesus died on the cross and was resurrected (raised from the dead) so we could be forgiven of our sins and receive eternal life.

It's just that simple because God doesn't make it hard for us. In order for you and I to be saved from the penalty of death, we have to be forgiven of our sins. *Forgiveness* means to be released or set free. Another way to describe forgiveness is to be "pardoned." It's like being convicted of the most horrible crime and being sentenced to death. I mean you committed the crime and you know you are guilty. However, when you go before the judge for sentencing, he delivers a verdict of "not guilty," and lets you off the hook. Because you knew you were guilty, you were expecting the book to be thrown at you. You're instantly relieved and you say to yourself softly while still in shock, "Maybe it's my lucky day!" However, the judge corrects you and says, "This has nothing to do with luck. There is no such thing. You see someone has to pay for what you've done. A price must be paid! You have been blessed! The only reason we are letting you go is because someone who loves you, in spite of your failures, has demanded that we let Him be put to death in your place. He has decided to pay the price for you so you could be released and set free." This is forgiveness. Jesus took the place of death for us so we could have the option to be saved and therefore, set free or forgiven of our sins.

You see, we were guilty as charged! Yet, Jesus bore the guilt and shame of our sins on the cross. He literally took it upon Himself. As a result, God has declared each person who receives Him as, "Not guilty!" Yes, I was guilty as charged, but through Him, I'm now, "Not guilty!"

Of Him all the prophets bear witness that through His name everyone who believes in Him receives forgiveness of sins. —Acts 10:43

And everyone who calls on the name of the Lord will be saved. —Act 2:21, niv

In him we have redemption through his blood, the forgiveness of sins, in accordance with the riches of God's grace. —Ephesians 1:7, niv

This whole concept of being forgiven is absolutely amazing. It's like having thousands upon thousands of dollars in debt that range from everything from student loans to credit card bills. Just imagine receiving a call from all your creditors explaining to you that someone has paid your obligations in full and therefore, your debt has been forgiven. Yes, your debt has been forgiven. You owed it, but now you don't. It's been forgiven! No more payments, no more headaches, no more fears. You're debt free! Jesus canceled the debt of eternal judgment stacked up against us and nailed it to the cross. Colossians 2:13–14 explains this: "When you were dead in your sins and in the uncircumcision of your sinful nature, God made you alive with Christ. He forgave us all our sins, having canceled the written code, with its regulations, that was against us and that stood opposed to us; he took it away, nailing it to the cross" (NIV).

Why did Jesus have to go through all that pain by dying on the cross the way He did in shedding His blood?

The reason that Jesus died a terrible death in shedding His blood is shown in the Bible. It says that there is no forgiveness of sin without the shedding of blood (Heb. 9:22). Back in the day, the only way that people had to make peace with God for their sins was to go to the temple and make a sacrifice. There were certain animals that you had to bring to be cleansed of different sins. Can you imagine how messy that got to be?

Do we have to offer up any more sacrifices to be forgiven of sin, whether that be the blood of animals or some other blood sacrifice that many religions practice?

The answer is no. Jesus Himself became the sacrifice for sin once and for all.

> Nor did he enter heaven to offer himself again and again, the way the high priest enters the Most Holy Place every year with blood that is not his own. Then Christ would have had to suffer many times since the creation of the world. But now he has appeared once for all at the end of the ages to do away with sin by the sacrifice of himself. Just as man is destined to die once, and after that to face judgment, so Christ was sacrificed once to take away the sins of many people; and he will appear a second time, not to bear sin, but to bring salvation to those who are waiting for him.
> —Hebrews 9:25–28, niv

Telling the Truth #5: Salvation is not earned; it is a free gift of God's grace.

Saved by Grace!

The great news is that God already knew that we couldn't live a perfect, sinless life by perfectly obeying the Ten Commandments or any other part of the Bible for that matter. He knew it. So He decided before the earth was even made to send His Son Jesus to live a perfect, sinless life on our behalf (1 Pet. 1:18–21). And therefore, qualifying Himself as the perfect sacrifice for our sins (2 Cor. 5:21). This is why Ephesians 1:7-10 says: "In him we have redemption through his blood, the forgiveness of sins, in accordance with the riches of God's grace that he lavished on us with all wisdom and understanding. And he made known to us the mystery of his will according to his good pleasure, which he purposed in Christ, to be put into effect when the times will have reached their fulfillment—to bring all things in heaven and on earth together under one head, even Christ" (niv).

What Is Grace?

The *Holman Bible Dictionary* defines *grace* as the undeserved acceptance and love received from another. This dictionary goes on to say that *grace* is synonymous with the gospel of God's gift of unmerited salvation in Jesus Christ. That means we didn't do anything to deserve it and there's nothing we can do to make Him take it away. Therefore, grace is not getting what I deserve; grace is getting what I don't deserve. I deserved eternal death as a payment for my sin, but I'm getting eternal life through faith in Christ Jesus. So I am saved not by works, anything I did or could do, but saved by grace based on God's unconditional love for me in everything He did in Christ on my behalf.

> But because of his great love for us, God, who is rich in mercy, made us alive with Christ even when we were dead in transgressions—it is by grace you have been saved. And God raised us up with Christ and seated us with him in the heavenly realms in Christ Jesus, in order that in the coming ages he might show the incomparable riches of his grace, expressed in his kindness to us in Christ Jesus. For it is by grace you have been saved, through faith—and this not from yourselves, it is the gift of God—not by works, so that no one can boast. —Ephesians 2:4–9, niv

God's gift of grace is the embodiment of the gospel rooted in His overwhelming feelings of love for you and me. This awesome grace of God is so much more than meets the eye!

Chapter 3

Out With the Old, in With the New!

And when He [Jesus] had taken some bread and given thanks, He broke it and gave it to them, saying, "This is My body which is given for you; do this in remembrance of Me." And in the same way He took the cup after they had eaten, saying, "This cup which is poured out for you is the new covenant in My blood. —Luke 22:19–20

For this is My blood of the covenant [speaking of the new covenant], which is poured out for many for forgiveness of sins. —Matthew 26:28

For you to understand the entire truth of the gospel, we need to expound on this whole idea of God's grace as it relates to sin. The best way to do that is to explain the differences between what the Bible calls the old covenant and the new covenant. *Covenant* simply means a binding agreement or promise usually under seal between two or more parties especially for the performance of some action (*Merriam-Webster Online Dictionary*). The old covenant is the agreement of laws that God made with His people in the Old Testament Bible days. The hallmark of the old covenant is The Ten Commandments. The new covenant is the agreement of grace that God has made with us through Jesus Christ. God initiated this new covenant for you, me, and everybody everywhere. Initiated means that it was His idea, He started it. Although God has made this new covenant available for everyone, it can be realized only by those who receive Jesus Christ. (See Chapter 6 for more details on receiving Jesus.)

When I accept Jesus into my life, I am no longer under the Law (old covenant), but under grace (new covenant). Under this new covenant of grace, I have specific promises from God that I can expect to receive. The main promise is in regard to sin. Under the new covenant, my sin is no longer taken into account, when I come to Jesus in *repentance*. *Repentance* means to confess (admit) your sin and commit to change. It is the act of turning from my sin and turning to God. I recently explained this concept to a college student who asked the question: "Does God show grace and forgive someone who has messed up big time, no matter the sin?" I answered: "Yes, God will absolutely pour out His grace and forgive anyone who *repents* of their sin." Notice that I said: "Anyone who *repents* of their sin."

> If we confess our sins, He [God] is faithful and righteous to forgive us our sins and to cleanse us from all unrighteousness. —1 John 1:9

Therefore, when I come to Jesus in repentance under this new covenant of grace, my sin doesn't count against me! That's right! It does not even count against me! Here's what the Bible says about this new covenant of grace: "Blessed are they whose transgressions are forgiven, whose sins are covered. Blessed is the man whose sin the Lord will never count against him" (Rom. 4:7–8, NIV).

Allow me to illustrate this point. Sometimes in football the offense will make a touchdown. But all of a sudden, in the middle of the end zone celebration, the referee waves off the touchdown because of a holding penalty. Yeah, it was an exciting run and the team got into the end zone, but it doesn't count. No points on the board and the whole play is wiped from the record. Or how about when you are playing hoops with your boys and somebody drives down the lane for the layup and they end up traveling. You know those games where that last bucket is the winning score and everybody is arguing over whether the guy traveled or not. "You traveled! That doesn't count!" And you're right. If he traveled, that last winning score, as pretty as it was, doesn't count at all. Not one bit!

When I sin as a believer (one who has received Jesus into their life), God does not count my sin against me. My slate stays clean before God and there is no record of my fall (sin). Because of my relationship with Jesus, I have gained access into a permanent grace under this new covenant, in which I now stand (Rom. 5:2). This grace in which I now stand is a continual forever state of being forgiven. I don't have to worry that I'm a "goner" if I don't ask the Lord to forgive me before I go to bed at night or as drastic as before I die. No, it doesn't work like that at all for me as a believer! I am already forgiven from the past, present, and future sins. Under this new promise in Jesus, I stand forgiven always!

So, if my sin doesn't count against me under this new covenant of grace, then does that mean I can just sin like crazy without any consequences?

If God is not taking my sin into account as a believer, then does that mean I can just go crazy and become sin city? That's not how it works. God's grace does not give you a license to sin. You can't think "I will do this even though I know it's wrong over and over again not because I'm struggling, but because I think I can get away with it." You see, God knows our hearts and He will not be mocked. It is true that what you sow you will reap. If your motive is to try to get over on God or "play" God, believe me when I tell you, it won't work. You can't "hustle" God! That is basically like spitting on this free gift of grace that He has given to you. The Lord knows those that are His. Those who in spite of their sins and failures have committed their lives to Him. These are the ones who truly have relationship with Him. When they fall, He picks them back up again. You see there is a difference between someone who is a Christian who is simply experiencing a sin struggle (the war between the flesh and spirit natures as outlined in Romans 6–7) and one who is not even on board with God. The person who isn't even on board with God has decided that the sin lifestyle is how they will live. Their theology is that since God loves everybody it's OK to just do whatever they want to do without any consequences. It's their life and their choice. Many in this group of people will call themselves Christians, but in reality, they are not!

> Do not let sin control the way you live; do not give in to its lustful desires. Do not let any part of your body become a tool of wickedness, to be used for sinning. Instead, give yourselves completely to God since you have been given new life. And use your whole body as a tool to do what is right for the glory of God. Sin is no longer your master, for you are no longer subject to the law, which enslaves you to sin. Instead, you are free by God's grace. So since God's grace has set us free from the law, does this mean we can go on sinning? Of course not!" —Romans 6:12–15, nlt

> Therefore do not let sin reign in your mortal body so that you obey its lusts, and do not go on presenting the members of your body to sin as instruments of unrighteousness; but present yourselves to God as those alive from the dead, and your members as instruments of righteousness to God. For sin shall not be master over you, *for you are not under law but under grace.* What then? Shall we sin because we are not under law but under grace? May it never be! —Romans 6:12–15, emphasis added

The Transition from the Old Covenant to the New Covenant (From the Law to Christ)

So this is the point: The law no longer holds you in its

power, because you died to its power when you died with Christ on the cross. And now you are united with the one who was raised from the dead. As a result, you can produce good fruit, that is, good deeds for God. When we were controlled by our old nature, sinful desires were at work within us, and the law aroused these evil desires that produced sinful deeds, resulting in death. But now we have been released from the law, for we died with Christ, and we are no longer captive to its power. Now we can really serve God, not in the old way by obeying the letter of the law, but in the new way, by the Spirit. Well then, am I suggesting that the law of God is evil? Of course not! The law is not sinful, but it was the law that showed me my sin. I would never have known that coveting is wrong if the law had not said, "Do not covet." But sin took advantage of this law and aroused all kinds of forbidden desires within me! If there were no law, sin would not have that power. I felt fine when I did not understand what the law demanded. But when I learned the truth, I realized I had broken the law and was a sinner, doomed to die. So the good law, which was supposed to show me the way of life, instead gave me the death penalty. Sin took advantage of the law and fooled me; it took the good law and used it to make me guilty of death. But still, the law itself is holy and right and good. —Romans 7:4–12, nlt

The people of Israel were the first people whom God chose to reveal Himself as Savior of the world in the Bible's Old Testament. The people of Israel were under the old covenant (the law). The old covenant included the Ten Commandments and other ordinances that God gave them to follow or to live by. The law in itself was holy, good, and right (Rom. 7:12). In fact, it made them aware of their sin, in the same way that it makes us aware of our sin today. For example, Romans 7:7 says, "I would never have known that coveting is wrong if the law had not said, 'You must not covet'"(nlt). The "You must not covet" commandment was the tenth commandment of the Old Testament Law. In the context of this law, it stated that it was wrong to covet someone else's belongings. For example, the commandment mentioned that it was wrong to covet your neighbor's house and your neighbor's wife (Exod. 20:17). Although the law in itself is holy, good, and right, when we are controlled by our sinful nature and sinful desires are at work in us, the law arouses these sinful desires. When the law arouses these sinful desires in us, we then fall into a lifestyle of sin (Rom. 7:5). As I mentioned in Chapter 2, a lifestyle of sin leads to death, eternal separation from God.

That is why God never designed the old covenant to be the final agreement between Him and us. The old covenant law was like a tutor that was intended to simply prepare the people of Israel for Jesus Christ.

> Therefore the Law has become our tutor to lead us to Christ, so that we may be justified by faith. — Galatians 3:24

The law was impossible to perfectly follow. If you broke one commandment, you were considered guilty of breaking the whole law (James 2:10). Therefore, the law became the tutor that pointed to our need for Christ—to save us from our sins, so that all of mankind would not suffer the penalty of death.

> I felt fine when I did not understand what the law demanded. But when I learned the truth, I realized I had broken the law and was a sinner, doomed to die. So the good law, which was supposed to show me the way of life, instead gave me the death penalty. — Romans 7:9–10, nlt

Jesus Christ came to earth and lived a perfect, sinless life, fulfilling the law on our behalf so that we could be made right with God, through faith in Him. Check out what Jesus said after His resurrection: Now He said to them, "These are My words which I spoke to you while I was still with you, that all things which are written about Me in the Law of Moses and the Prophets and the Psalms must be fulfilled." Then He opened their minds to understand the Scriptures, and He said to them, "Thus it is written, that the Christ would suffer and rise again from the dead the third day, and that repentance for forgiveness of sins would be proclaimed in His name to all the nations, beginning from Jerusalem" (Luke 24:44–47).

OK, now let's look back at Romans 7. The writer explains to the people that when they received Jesus, they were joined with Him. He goes on to explain that just as Christ died, they too have now died to the law, being released from its power (Rom. 7:4). It was important for them to be released from the power of the law because, as I mentioned, if they broke just even one commandment, they were guilty of death. Our relationship with God through His Son, Jesus Christ, has put away the old way of serving God and brought us into the *new way* of serving God. This new way of serving God is through the *Spirit* of God in us by faith in Jesus Christ.

> But now we have been released from the law, for we died with Christ, and we are no longer captive to its power. Now we can really serve God, not in the old way by obeying the letter of the law, but in the new way, by the *Spirit.* —Romans 7:6, nlt, emphasis added

The reality is that when I receive Jesus into my life, I am born again and His Spirit, the Spirit of God, aka the Holy Spirit, comes and lives on the inside of me.

> Jesus replied, "I assure you, unless you are born again, you can never see the Kingdom of God." "What do you mean?" exclaimed Nicodemus. "How can an old man go back into his mother's womb and be born again?" Jesus replied, "The truth is, no one can enter

the Kingdom of God without being born of water and the *Spirit*. Humans can reproduce only human life, but the *Holy Spirit* gives new life from heaven. So don't be surprised at my statement that you must be born again. Just as you can hear the wind but can't tell where it comes from or where it is going, so you can't explain how people are *born of the Spirit*." —John 3:3–8, nlt

I will ask the Father, and He will give you another *Helper*, that He may be with you forever; that is the *Spirit of truth*, whom the world cannot receive [referring to people who do not receive Jesus], because it does not see Him or know Him, but you know Him because He abides with you and will be in you [referring to people who receive Jesus]. —John 14:16–17, emphasis added

Under grace (the new covenant). Jesus is in me, the treasure in earthen vessels (2 Cor. 4:7). Therefore, Jesus lives His life through me, while doing His good works. That's why the Bible says, "And now you are united with the one who was raised from the dead [Jesus]. As a result, you can produce good fruit, that is, good deeds for God" (Rom. 7:4, nlt).

But the fruit of the Spirit is love, joy, peace, patience, kindness, goodness, faithfulness, gentleness, self-control; against such things there is no law. —Galatians 5:22–23

OLD vs. NEW

Old Covenant	New Covenant
1. Moses was the mediator	1. Jesus is the mediator
2. Priest had to offer up a yearly sacrifice for the sin of himself and all the people	2. Jesus became the sacrifice for all sin once and for all
3. Gave no way out from the fear of punishment	3. Gives me forgivness through the perfect love of Jesus that gets rid of all fear
4. Resulted in death	4. Results in life and freedom
5. Each male had to be circumcised	5. God circumcises the heart
6. Based on performance (human effort)	6. Based on grace through faith in Jesus Christ
7. Righteousness can never be realized	7. I am the righteousness of God in Christ Jesus

Let's look at each one carefully to see the real deal behind these differences.

Old Covenant	New Covenant
1. Moses was the mediator	1. Jesus is the mediator
2. Priest had to offer up a yearly sacrifice for the sin of himself and all the people	2. Jesus became the sacrifice for all sin once and for all

For this reason Christ is the mediator of a *new covenant*, that those who are called may receive the promised eternal inheritance—now that he has died as a ransom to set them free from the sins committed under the first covenant. —Hebrews 9:15, niv, emphasis added

For the law was given through Moses; *grace* and truth came through Jesus Christ—John 1:17, niv, emphasis added

When people sinned under the old covenant, the priest had to offer up a yearly sacrifice (for example, lamb) for his sin and for the sins of all the people. This is how God commanded Moses, the chosen mediator of the law, to do it. The term *mediator* is defined as a peacemaker, a negotiator who establishes a certain relationship, or a neutral person who can guarantee an agreement (*Holman Bible Dictionary*). Therefore, it was never a permanent solution because it had to be done each year in order for peace to be made between the people and God. Under the new covenant, Jesus, as the mediator, became the sacrifice for all sin once and for all (Heb. 10:10–12). All those who receive Him are forgiven once and for all of all sin. That includes your past, present, and future sins. And take in mind that when I'm truly forgiven, I no longer bear the guilt and shame that comes with committing that act. The slate is wiped clean and remains clean. This new covenant that was sealed by the finished work of Jesus Christ on the cross (by the shedding of His blood) completely eliminates the guilt and shame experienced from the effects of sin. That's why the Hebrew writer strongly encourages the believer with these words:

> And so, dear brothers and sisters, we can boldly enter heaven's Most Holy Place because of the blood of Jesus. This is the new, life-giving way that Christ has opened up for us through the sacred curtain, by means of His death for us. And since we have a great High Priest [Jesus] who rules over God's people, Let us go right into the presence of God, with true hearts fully trusting Him. For our evil consciences have been sprinkled with Christ blood to make us clean, and our bodies have been washed with pure water. —Hebrews 10:19–22, nlt

> Therefore, brothers, since we have confidence to enter the Most Holy Place by the blood of Jesus, by a new and living way opened for us through *the curtain, that*

is, his body, and since we have a great priest [Jesus] over the house of God, let us draw near to God with a sincere heart in full assurance of faith, having our hearts sprinkled to cleanse us from a *guilty conscience* and having our bodies washed with pure water. — Hebrews 10:19–22, niv, emphasis added

Old Covenant	New Covenant
3. Gave no way out from the fear of punishment	3. Gives me forgivness through the perfect love of Jesus that gets rid of all fear
4. Resulted in death	4. Results in life and freedom

Yeah, that's right. You see, since the old covenant does not provide a way for us to have our sins completely paid for, we are stuck. The law does not and cannot give me a solution to be forgiven of my sin once and for all. Therefore, I am stuck with the "leftovers" of the fear of punishment. It's thinking, "If I do this, then this bad thing will happen to me." Let me explain how this works in an everyday example we can all relate to. Often times when I'm running late I tend to get a heavy foot even though I know I shouldn't. When I'm speeding, I'm thinking that everything is cool and that there's nothing to worry about. "I'm just driving a little fast; it's all good." But as soon as that police car appears seemingly out of nowhere, I and everybody else on the road start slowing down in a hurry! My heart starts pounding while I'm praying that his siren doesn't go off and come in my direction. "Please Lord, don't let me get a ticket. Please let him just keep driving." The reason why I and everybody else slowed down was because we were afraid of being punished for our actions. In this case, it's breaking the speeding law. The police are there to enforce the law and you don't want to get into trouble. If you go over the speed limit, you will be judged and incur the penalty of getting a ticket.

This same fear of punishment is at work for those under the old covenant law, but on a whole other level. Here's the kicker. When people broke the Old Testament laws, they could legally be stoned to death. But when Jesus came on the scene with His new covenant of grace, He said that He desires compassion instead.

> "But go and learn what this means: 'I DESIRE COMPASSION, AND NOT SACRIFICE,' for I did not come to call the righteous, but sinners." — Matthew 9:13

This was Jesus's attitude. It was His heart. It was how He "rolled." And let me tell you, Jesus was and still is relentless with His grace. He expressed it to everyone that He came in contact with no matter who they were. He loved on people showing them His compassion, mercy and grace to the fullest! One prime example of this is seen in a true story recorded in the Bible about a woman caught in the act of adultery. Under the law, this was actually a crime that was worthy of death. That means that they could legally stone this women to death for what she did. To put it to you straight, she was actually sentenced to the death penalty for committing the crime of sleeping around! And let me tell you, she would have gotten the death penalty if Jesus had not showed up. In John 8, the teachers of the law brought her in and set her in front of everybody in the center court (John 8:3). Just think how guilty, humiliated and embarrassed she must have felt. They put her business in the street in front of everybody! After they accused her of her crime, they tried to test Jesus by asking His opinion of what should be done with the woman (John 8:5–6). All the while reminding Him that under the law given by Moses she was supposed to be killed, no questions asked! And they were right according to the law because that's exactly what it says in the seventh commandment. But check out how Jesus mixes things up after they kept bugging Him to give them an answer:

When they kept on questioning him, he straightened

up and said to them, "If any one of you is without sin, let him be the first to throw a stone at her." —John 8:7, niv

The Bible says that when they heard Him say this, they began to bounce one by one beginning with the older ones (John 8:9). After a statement like that, who could still stand there trying to accuse her. Nobody! Why? Because each one of them standing in judgment against this woman had some skeletons of their own in their closets. They knew that they too had sinned and would not want to be put to death for the sins that they had committed. In that moment, we see the better covenant of grace at work. You see, Jesus was more concerned about helping people and restoring them even if it meant breaking the rules. You can be doing the right things and following the rules and still be wrong in your response to people. The religious parties of their day had this down pat. But Jesus introduced a new covenant that focused on loving people above the rules. Jesus never judged the woman even though out of all of the people present He was the one who could have judged her and been justified. Still, He didn't do it. I think that He could have judged her because He was the only one in the room without sin. But nope, He didn't judge her, not for one second! Jesus forgave the woman, accepted her where she was, loved her unconditionally in the midst of her mess, and gave her an out from her lifestyle of sin for a new life of relationship with God. This was a true act of grace! This is what grace is all about.

At this, those who heard began to go away one at a time, the older ones first, until only Jesus was left, with the woman still standing there. Jesus straightened up and asked her, "Woman, where are they? Has no one condemned you?" "No one, sir," she said. "Then neither do I condemn you," Jesus declared. "Go now and leave your life of sin." —John 8:9–11, niv

Under the new covenant, you do not have a fear of punishment because Jesus conquered death for you so you could inherit eternal life. This story shows us a picture of the new covenant. By law, she was supposed to be put to death, but Jesus saved her! Jesus died in our place because by law, we, like this woman, should be put to death for our sins. He has set us free from the fear of death when we accept His death, His sacrifice for us. When we accept Him and all that He did for us on the cross, we receive life in Him. Therefore in Jesus, I now have the promise of life and freedom. His perfect love gets rid of all fear! You don't have to be afraid anymore. After receiving Christ, you can read some of God's promises to you, His child, and apply them to your life. If you feel afraid of death, you can read Romans 8:35–39, which says that nothing, not even death itself, can separate us from the love of God in Christ Jesus. Or read 1 John 4:14–19, which affirms the fact that those who accept the love of God through Christ Jesus will not undergo any punishment.

Therefore, you can live your life in His perfect peace instead of having the fear of death and punishment hanging over your head. God promises that all who receive His Son, Jesus, can stand before Him on judgment day with confidence! Before receiving Christ, you couldn't help but fear death because deep in your spirit, you knew you were not right with God. Now, you can choose to accept His truth and enjoy a life that is free from the spirit of fear and the fear of death and punishment. You have nothing to fear anymore. When you die, you'll spend eternity with Him in perfect peace. You've been saved from the torment for your sins. And let me add something else. It's important for everyone to know that since Jesus has provided a way out from the penalty of our sin, we don't have to be ruled by what I call the "judge alarm." This is the alarm that goes off inside your head when you mess up or blow it. You start judging and beating yourself up over your mistakes. You think, "How could I do that!" "I'm such a bad person!" "What's wrong with me?" "I can't believe I did that!" Under the new covenant, the "judge alarm" is smashed under the feet of grace and thrown out the window and replaced with the "alarm of mercy." The question is, "Which alarm are you responding to today?" If it is the alarm of judgment, I invite you into this new covenant of grace where the wake-up call of mercy rings true every time without fail! It is all set by the God of mercy, my Lord and Savior Jesus Christ, praise be to God!

> "For God did not send the Son into the world to judge the world, but that the world might be saved through Him." —John 3:17

Since the result of the new covenant of grace is life and freedom, I am free from the obsolete thinking of the old covenant. I can relax and rest in the grace of God being absolutely free from a works mentality of somehow trying to earn my salvation. I don't have to try to get ahead, I'm already ahead in Jesus.

Old Covenant	New Covenant
5. Each male had to be circumcised	5. God circumcises the heart

For those of you who like me didn't know where the tradition of circumcision came from, let me explain. Under the old covenant it was required by God that each male be circumcised. This was the sign to show that they were in covenant with God. This is what I call the "mark" from that time period (before the coming of Jesus and the new covenant) that proved you were right with God and His covenant with you. In contrast, under the new covenant, the sign or mark to show you are right with God is faith in Jesus Christ who performs a circumcision on your heart. Of course I don't mean Jesus is going to give you a physical heart transplant. It is more in the context of a spiritual heart transplant.

Think of it this way. Your heart refers to your mind and soul. First, this includes your way of thinking, your thought life, and attitudes. Second, it includes your decision-making, your will, your desires (for example, lusts), and conscience. Third, it includes your emotions or feelings. It is your true self or nature. The behaviors or actions you choose in life are based on this nature of your heart. Jesus said in His Word that when we didn't know Him, our hearts were completely based in the sinful nature to the point where we just naturally followed its lust and desires without question (as explained in Chapter 2). Matthew 15:19 quotes Jesus as saying, "From the heart come evil thoughts, murder, adultery, all other sexual immorality, theft, lying, and slander" (NLT). Therefore, each one of us has a heart that is in a bad condition as a result of its sinful nature. This spiritual fact makes us all prime candidates for a heart transplant from Jesus. This is what takes place under the new covenant when we receive Jesus into our lives. We receive a circumcision done by Christ that "cuts away" this sinful nature.

> When you came to Christ, you were "circumcised," but not by a physical procedure. It was a spiritual procedure—the cutting away of your sinful nature. For you were buried with Christ when you were baptized. And with Him you were raised to a new life because you trusted the mighty power of God, who raised Christ from the dead. You were dead because of your sins and because your sinful nature was not yet cut away. Then God made you alive with Christ. He forgave all our sins. —Colossians 2:11–13, nlt

Now don't get me wrong, there is nothing wrong with the physical circumcision. However, as it relates to my relationship with God, it's not about the circumcision of the body, but about my faith in Jesus Christ who has circumcised my heart. I have a new way of thinking according to His ways, thoughts and character. I have a new way of relating to Him. Not as I saw Him before as the God ready to punish me if I broke the law, sinned, and made a mistake. But as the God who loves me by His awesome mercy and grace.

What's the problem with trying to stay under the old covenant now that the new covenant has been established?

The problem for us today with trying to stay under this old covenant now that the new covenant exists is really simple. God has given us the new covenant and specifically states that it is a replacement of the old. As soon as He established the new covenant through Jesus, He made the old covenant obsolete. *Obsolete* means you can't use it anymore, it just won't work.

When He said, "A new covenant," He has made the first obsolete. But whatever is becoming obsolete and growing old is ready to disappear. — Hebrews 8:13

When God speaks of a new covenant, it means He has made the first one obsolete. It is now out of date and ready to be put aside. — Hebrews 8:13, nlt

In fact, the Bible describes the new covenant as being a better covenant based on better promises (Heb. 8:6). Another reason you can't try to stay under the old covenant is because no matter how hard you try, you can't live up to keeping the law perfectly. Don't forget that Jesus said that if you break the law in your heart, you're guilty of sin (As described in Chapter 2).

Old Covenant	New Covenant
6. Based on performance (human effort)	6. Based on grace through faith in Jesus Christ

If I could just, forgive myself!

I can remember the stage of my life after I had recently given my heart to Jesus as a new Christian. God had given me a newfound peace and joy that I had never experienced before and He was doing some great things in our relationship. After

I had received Jesus, I knew that God had forgiven me of all my past, present, and future sin, but I still struggled with this reality in my heart. In other words, I struggled greatly with forgiving myself when I messed up or made a mistake. This pattern went on for a while when I would feel great if I had a "good day" and I would feel bad if I had a "bad day." What I didn't realize at the time is that even though I was saved and going to heaven, I didn't have an accurate view of God and how He saw me, especially when I sinned. I knew in my mind that God loved me, but for some reason, it had not entirely penetrated my heart (in respect to how I felt about myself).

However, one day during a drive on the local parkway, things began to change. I had experienced what I called a "bad day" and as usual, I was feeling bad and beating myself up about it. During my drive, I started listening to the Christian radio station and the broadcast of Dr. Charles Stanley. I didn't catch the title of the sermon because when I tuned in, the program was already in progress. Nevertheless, I remember feeling like God was talking directly to me through this broadcast. Dr. Stanley spoke about our new position in Christ as the believer and how our sin is under the blood of Jesus. He encouraged the listeners to forgive themselves just as God had done, and that sanctification was a process. I felt so liberated in that moment! God had spoken His truth to me and then He began to build on that foundation. I later learned that people who have experienced an abusive childhood, like me, often develop a false view of God without even realizing it. For example, if you were abused by an authority figure (e.g., a parent), then you tend to view God as one who is easily angered and ready to punish you when you blow it.

In my case, my brother and I had been severely abused physically and verbally by our first stepmother. We experienced this abuse without my father's knowledge. In addition to this, I was separated from my natural mother when I was approximately five years old and I didn't see her again until I was twenty-one. The vicious cycle of all of these events caused me to have a very painful childhood while tainting my "God view" in the process. Many people struggle with these false views of God. Even though they know differently, what they really believe about God (in their subconscious) will often be demonstrated through their actions. The more God began to heal me from the scars of my abuse and I continued to grow in my relationship with Him, the more I truly understood this new covenant of grace that we have in Jesus. I learned that it wasn't so much about my sin, as much as it was about how I viewed God. I began to experience a different focus in life under this new covenant of grace.

I realized *in my heart* that God was not out to change my behavior, but that His only motive was to capture my heart. I also learned that after He had my heart, He (by His Holy Spirit in me) would help me overcome the sin struggles in my life. The reason Jesus wanted to help me overcome my sin struggles was not because He wanted to "fix" me or make me a "good person." The reason was because He loved me so much that He wanted to help me change the destructive patterns in my life that were hurting me and my relationships. As a result, I developed a healthy, accurate view of God and how He felt about me. I died to a *performance-based mentality* and entered into the *new covenant grace mentality* in Jesus Christ. The focus is His grace, not my sin. My sin is covered and the life I now live in the body is unto the Lord Jesus Christ.

Maybe your story isn't quite as traumatic as mine, but you can definitely relate to what I am saying. Perhaps, you struggle with forgiving yourself. Maybe you are a new Christian or you've been saved for years, but you still can't seem to change this false view of God. Well, there is hope! In the following segment, I will explain the difference between the *performance-based mentality* in your relationship with God and the *new covenant grace mentality* in your relationship with God. Secondly, I will expose the lie of the performance-based mentality through what I've entitled "The Performance Quiz."

Telling the Truth #6: I am right (in perfect standing) with God through faith in Jesus Christ *alone*.

Performance-Based Mentality vs. New Covenant Grace Mentality

How does this affect me today in my relationship with God?

Performance-Based Mentality (false view of God): "If I'm a good person and I do what's right the majority of the time, I am right with God."

New Covenant Grace Mentality (accurate view of God): "I am right with God through faith in Jesus Christ *alone*."

The *new covenant* is based on grace through faith in Jesus Christ. Let me explain how this truth applies to your everyday life. Under the *new covenant*, I don't relate to God based on my performance (my behavior and the things I do) of meeting the rules and regulations of religion. I relate to God based on His grace through my relationship with His Son, Jesus Christ. This new covenant puts an end to the mind-set that my good standing with God is fulfilled by obeying the "do's and don'ts" that I call my performance. Under this new covenant, my perspective completely changes because God gives me a new heart and a new way of thinking.

If the first covenant had been faultless, there would have been no need for a second covenant to replace it. But God found fault with the people and said: "The time is coming, declares the Lord, when I will make a new covenant with the house of Israel and with the house of Judah. This covenant will not be like the one I made with their ancestors [speaking of the old covenant] when I took them by the hand and led them out of the land of Egypt. They did not remain faithful to my covenant [the old covenant], so I turned my back on them, says the Lord. But this is the new covenant I will make with the people of Israel on that day, says the Lord: I will put My laws in their minds so they will understand them, and I will write them on their hearts so they will obey them. I will be their God, and they will be my people. And they will not need to teach their neighbors, nor will they need to teach their family, saying, 'You should know the Lord.' For everyone, from the least to the greatest, will already know Me. And I will forgive their wrongdoings, and I will never again remember their sin.'" —Hebrews 8:7–12, nlt

For if there had been nothing wrong with that first covenant, no place would have been sought for another. *But God found fault with the people and said: "The time is coming, declares the Lord, when I will make a new covenant with the house of Israel and with the house of Judah.* It will not be like the covenant I made with their forefathers when I took them by the hand to lead them out of Egypt, because they did not remain faithful to my covenant, and I turned away from them, declares the Lord. This is the covenant I will make with the house of Israel after that time, declares the Lord. I will put my laws in their minds and write them on their hearts. I will be their God, and they will be my people. No longer will a man teach his neighbor, or a man his brother, saying, 'Know the Lord,' because they will all know me, from the least of them to the greatest. For I will forgive their wickedness and will remember their sins no more." —Hebrews 8:7–12, niv, emphasis added

As stated above, under the new covenant, God promises me that He will "tattoo" His ways on my heart and mind.

The Performance Quiz: How do I know if I'm living my life under a performance-based mentality opposed to a *new covenant* grace mentality?

Key: A performance-based mentality relates to my behavior and the things I do.

1. It relates to your relationship with God and how He sees you.

When I do good (works, behavior), God is pleased with me. For example, when you do good (or do good things), you feel like those works earn you a spot in heaven or maybe a good position with God. You think, "I'm cool with God because I do x, y, and z."

However, when I do "bad" (sin behavior), God is mad at me. Here's what this looks like. As a person (Christian or not), do you find yourself avoiding or running away from God when you blow it, instead of running to Him through prayer?

2. It relates to how you see or feel about yourself.

When I do good (works, behavior), I feel better about myself as a person and sometimes it leads to pride or thinking too highly of myself. For example, do you find yourself feeling like you're a good person only when you're doing good things? But somehow you feel depressed and down when you're doing things you perceive to be bad? It's almost like in those moments, you truly feel like you're a bad person. Or do you find yourself bragging and boasting about what you do for people to the point that you start to feel better than other people? You even compare yourself to others and judge them by your works and how well they know God by their good works.

When I do bad (sin behavior), I feel terrible about myself. Does your life or relationship with God feel like a roller coaster? Up and down, up and down? When you sin do you keep asking God to forgive you over and over again because you really don't believe that He has? I can tell you that one of the reasons you struggle with this is because you honestly have a hard time forgiving yourself. I feel you. As I mentioned, I've been there!

When you sin, do you feel distant from God and people, and think, "I'm no good today" or "I'm not a Christian today." I mean, you know in your mind that God loves you, but you feel a gap between Him and you when you make a mistake. When you are in this state, you often struggle with condemnation, and your mistakes continue to replay in your mind over and over again.

Lastly, when you sin, do you feel like you have to get saved all over again? It's like you just don't feel good enough, so you have to start over every time. Well, if you can relate or identify with any of these questions and statements, then you are probably experiencing a performance-based lifestyle that God does not desire for you. Don't sweat it though because just about all of us have experienced this in our lives. In fact, most people (Christian or not) are experiencing it right now and don't even know it. They just don't recognize it. It's kind of like a "blind spot" of religion. Performance-based thinking can be overcome only by the acceptance of the *new covenant* of grace that we now have through faith in Jesus Christ.

This grace is experienced through a revelation of Jesus Christ from relationship with Him. If you've got Jesus, you've got a wide-open door to His awesome grace. It's available. The truth is that somebody just had to stop by to let you know it's there for you. It's right there waiting, with your name on it! Let's pray. *Lord, I pray that you would heal each person from the scars of abuse and religion. I ask that you would set them free from the lie of this performance-based mind-set. I pray that you would give them a true revelation of You, Jesus Christ, and Your love for them under Your new covenant. Thank you, God, for erasing the false views of You that they once had and for giving them an accurate view of who You really are. I pray that this accurate view would penetrate their hearts and allow them to see themselves the way you see them—with eyes of unconditional love and grace!*

Stand Firm in the Grace of God!

As a result of reading this book, many of you will come to Jesus. Please be careful that after you have received Jesus that you remain in His new covenant grace. I am encouraging you because a lot of seasoned Christians and churches with good intentions will try to indoctrinate you with their religious thinking, which consists of man-made ideas, rules, and regulations about God, but they are not from God. Therefore, their religious mind-set has given them inaccurate views of God that are often performance-based. This religious thinking will frequently come across in their teaching because they do not understand God's new covenant of grace and our new position in Christ. Please respect them and keep in mind that we are all in this together and that we are all on the same team. Also remember that most of us experienced this same blind spot until God revealed it to us Himself, or someone came along to teach us the entire truth about God's grace. When we learn the truth about grace, we receive a revelation of Jesus that enables us to overcome the lie of performance. Therefore, in love, pray that the church would accept this new covenant of grace that we now have in Christ Jesus.

> Therefore, since we have been justified through faith, we have peace with God through our Lord Jesus Christ, through whom we have gained access by faith into this grace in which we now stand. And we rejoice in the hope of the glory of God. —Romans 5:1–2, niv

> So Christ has really set us free. Now make sure you stay free, and don't get tied up again in slavery to the law. —Galatians 5:1, nlt

Old Covenant	New Covenant
7. Righteousness can never be realized	7. I am the righteousness of God in Christ Jesus

OK, let's get down to the nitty-gritty here about this whole righteousness business and what it truly means. My definition of righteousness is to be right with God relationally, completely reconciled. To be right with God is to be at peace with Him. Are you at peace with your Maker? The only way to be cool with God is through faith in Jesus Christ.

> It was for us, too, assuring us that God will also declare us to be righteous if we believe in God, who brought Jesus our Lord back from the dead. He was handed over to die because of our sins, and He was raised from the dead to make us right with God. —Romans 4:24–25, nlt

> Therefore, since we have been justified [made right in God's sight] through faith, we have peace with God through our Lord Jesus Christ, through whom we have gained access by faith into this grace [the new covenant we've been talking about] in which we now stand." —Romans 5:1–2, niv

Therefore, it's clear that righteousness cannot be achieved by following the law (old covenant). Never ever, ever! Since this is a hard-core fact, then that means that you cannot be saved by the law. You can be saved only by grace, through faith in Jesus Christ.

The first time I explained my personal experience of finally being right with God was during a family visit at my parents' home in Denver. It was late and my parents had gone to bed. But Melanie, one of my brothers, his wife, my twin brother, and I were still up. We were all together in my parents' den having one of those late-night conversations. That night and throughout the day, my brother's wife had kept saying to us that I was very different from how she remembered me when we were growing up. You see, back in the day, I dated her very close friend, who she always introduced as her cousin. I guess you could say she was her "play cousin" since technically they weren't really cousins. These two girls and my brother and I spent a lot of time together. So, she knew me well! Now, when she said how different I looked she kind of phrased it like it was the same me, but the person underneath was totally different.

I knew exactly what she meant because this was the first time she had seen me since I had accepted Jesus into my life. They knew the old me but not the "born again" new me. I explained what, or should I say Who, the difference was (Jesus), as I shared my faith with them. My heart went out to them because we all used to run together, each one of us side by side, living the same lie. In that conversation, I talked about how when I received Jesus, I was transferred from the kingdom of darkness (under Satan) to the kingdom of light of God's dear Son, Jesus Christ (Col. 1:13). I told them that I had been given a new position in Christ and therefore, I was now finally right with God. I pointed out that under this new position, when we sin or mess up, it is not taken into account because God sees me as "not guilty." I am "not guilty" because of the blood of Jesus that was shed for me. This is what it also means to be righteous or cool with God. Even though you are guilty of sin, God has forever forgiven you, sanctified you, and made you righteous. He has declared you as "not guilty!" This is my reality as the believer.

When I had not accepted God's Son, I did not truly know God. I would sin and still be in the guilty category, because of that sin. But now, by God's grace, He has changed my position with Him to the "right" category—no longer guilty of sin. This is the amazing grace of God! All I have to do is accept Him and everything changes. He has literally done me the biggest favor of my life. That night I told my family that I no longer have to work for it or try to earn it in any way, shape, form, or fashion. No matter how hard you might try, you can never be right with God without Jesus. It is only through Jesus that we have peace with God (Rom. 5:1). Things have been made right between us. I am reconciled to God and therefore the righteousness of God in Christ Jesus.

He made Him [Jesus] who knew no sin to be sin on our behalf, so that we might become the righteousness of God in Him. —2 Corinthians 5:21

For God made Christ, who never sinned, to be the offering for our sin, so that we could be made right with God through Christ. —2 Corinthians 5:21, nlt

Since I am the righteousness of God in Christ Jesus, then the truth according to God is that I am just as righteous as He is. Not because of anything I did to earn or deserve it, but because of what He did for me as a free gift of His grace.

Chapter 4

Who Is Jesus?

Telling the Truth #7: Jesus is God.

Yes, Jesus is God, hands down. This is the truth, but please let me prove it to you so that you can see it for yourself. Let's start by looking at the following conversation between Jesus and one of His disciples (followers) in the Book of John:

> "If you really knew me, you would know my Father as well. From now on, you do know him and have seen him." Philip said, "Lord, show us the Father and that will be enough for us." Jesus answered: "Don't you know me, Philip, even after I have been among you such a long time? Anyone who has seen me has seen the Father. How can you say, 'Show us the Father'? Don't you believe that I am in the Father, and that the Father is in me? The words I say to you are not just my own. Rather, it is the Father, living in me, who is doing his work. Believe me when I say that I am in the Father and the Father is in me; or at least believe on the evidence of the miracles themselves. —John 14:7–11, niv

Here we see the conversation between Jesus and Philip about Jesus's identity. You see Jesus was telling Philip that knowing Him meant knowing God (the Father). Jesus went on to explain to Philip that when they saw Him they were seeing God. However, like most of us, when we first hear this truth ("Help us Lord!"), Philip had a hard time believing it.

We see this disbelief when Philip asked Jesus to show him and the other disciples God right after Jesus already said that He is God. The following includes the dialogue between Jesus and Philip in John 14:7–11 paraphrased in my own words:

Jesus: Philip look no further, I am yours truly, the One and Only God. When you look at Me, you see God.

Philip: Uhhh, Jesus I know you say that you are God and that when we look at You, we are seeing Him. But really, come on now. Stop playing. Show us God and then everything will be cool.

Jesus: Philip, you're kidding right? I have spent all this time with you and you still don't know who I am? OK. If you find it hard to believe that the Father and I are the same person, then at least believe based on all the miracles you've seen Me do with your own eyes!

This is so funny when you think about it. I thank God for the Philips in the Bible because we see that Jesus's disciples were just like us, average human beings. That gives us hope.

OK, a lot of you are seeing the truth that Jesus is God. However, I have a feeling that some of you are still not sure, yet. So I'll give you more proof. Here we go; check out what the Book of John has to say in Chapter 1:

In the beginning was the Word, and the Word was with God, and the Word was God. He was with God in the beginning. Through him all things were made; without him nothing was made that has been made. In him was life, and that life was the light of men. —John 1:1–4, niv

He was in the world, and though the world was made through him, the world did not recognize him. He came to that which was his own, but his own did not receive him. Yet to all who received him, to those who believed in his name, he gave the right to become children of God—children born not of natural descent, nor of human decision or a husband's will, but born of God. The Word became flesh and made his dwelling among us. We have seen his glory, the glory of the One and Only, who came from the Father, full of grace and truth. —John 1:10–14, niv

Now, I can just see some of ya'll thinking, "What? What does this mean?" It's OK, flow with me as I explain. I first need to lay a foundation or give you the backbone to this thing. In verse 1, "In the beginning" refers to the beginning of time as we know it recorded in the Book of Genesis. The scripture is telling us that in the beginning, God created everything (the heaven and earth) by His Word. In other words, whatever God spoke came into existence when He said it by His Word. Let me show you so you can fully understand the scriptures. Let's go to the Book of Genesis and start reading from the very beginning in Chapter 1:

In the beginning God created the heavens and the earth. Now the earth was formless and empty, darkness was over the surface of the deep, and the Spirit of God was hovering over the waters. And God said, "Let there be light," and there was light. God saw that the light was good, and He separated the light from the darkness. God called the light "day," and the darkness he called "night." And there was evening, and there was morning—the first day. And God said, "Let there be an expanse between the waters to separate water from water." So God made the expanse and separated the water under the expanse from the water above it. And it was so. God called the expanse "sky." And there was evening, and there was morning—the second day. And God said, "Let the water under the sky be gathered to one place, and let dry ground appear." And it was so.

God called the dry ground "land," and the gathered waters he called "seas." And God saw that it was good. —Genesis 1:1–10, niv

Now, if you were to keep reading this chapter, you would see that it continues on with the phrase "God said" each time God created something. This phrase is very important to understand because everything created by God was first spoken or "said" by God, by His Word. In just looking at what we read, God created day, night, the sky, land, and seas, all spoken by His Word. God said it and bam!! There it was! OK now look back at the first part of John Chapter 1. I want to point out some very important facts about this passage:

Fact 1: The Word is referring to a person (It says "He" in John 1:2).

Fact 2: Jesus is the Word (John 1:14–18).

Fact 3: When the scripture says in John 1:1 that the Word (Jesus) was with God, its simply telling us that God and His Word (Jesus) are one in the same. In other words, God and Jesus are the same person. Therefore, you cannot separate God from His Word (Jesus). I want you to think of it like this. Let's say you make the following statement to your friends, "I'm going to the movies and you guys can come with me." Now, if I were to ask your friends who told them they could go to the movies with you, they would say that you did. They wouldn't separate you from what you said because when you say something, it's you talking. In other words, you can't separate you from your words. In the same way, you can't separate God from His Word (Jesus); they are one.

Fact 4: God came to earth as the Man, Jesus. John 1:14 says, "the Word became flesh and made his dwelling among us" (niv).

Fact 5: Jesus is 100 percent God and 100 percent man in one body.

I and the Father are One. — John 10–30, niv

Telling the Truth #8: Jesus is the Lamb of God.

In Bible times, lambs were sacrificed (killed as an offering to God) by the priest to make "atonement" for the sins of the people and himself (Lev. 16:32–34, 17:11). The sins of the people and the priest separated them from God. As part of their custom, on a certain day of each year called, the Day of Atonement, the priest would offer up this lamb sacrifice to God so they would be cleansed from their sin and reconciled back to God. You see as a result of their yearly sacrifice, God forgave them of their sins and it reconciled, or what I call "fixed the broken relationship," each year between them and God. But Jesus became the human sacrifice sent by God to cleanse us all from our sins and reconcile us back to Himself. That is why He is referred to as the Lamb of God.

> The next day John [a great man of God whom God said was the greatest of all the prophets] saw Jesus coming toward Him and said, "Look, the Lamb of God, who takes away the sin of the world!" —John 1:29, niv

The price that Jesus paid was done once and for all. Therefore, Jesus did away with the burdensome need to offer up a yearly sacrifice to be "cool" or "right" with God. You receive Jesus once and you are cool with God forever. And as I say all the time to the teenagers that I speak to, "Our relationship with God was broken and Jesus came to fix it!" This is what reconciliation means in plain terms. Jesus, the Lamb of God, came to literally reconcile us back to God. He came to fix the broken relationship between Him and us.

> Therefore if anyone is in Christ, he is a new creature; the old things passed away; behold, new things have come. Now all these things are from God, who reconciled us to Himself through Christ and gave us the ministry of reconciliation, namely, that God was in Christ reconciling the world to Himself, not counting their trespasses [sins] against them, and

He has committed to us the word of reconciliation. Therefore, we are ambassadors for Christ, as though God were making an appeal through us; we beg you on behalf of Christ, be reconciled to God. He made Him who knew no sin to be sin on our behalf, so that we might become the righteousness of God in Him. —2 Corinthians 5:17–21

Why did God come in the form of the man, Jesus?

Have your ever heard the phrase, "If you want something done right, then you need to do it yourself?" Well, that is exactly what God did. He loved us so much that He voluntarily came down from heaven to earth in the form of a man to pay the price for our sin (death). He literally took on humanity, knowing from the very beginning that He was going to die a painful death on our behalf. Jesus experienced the same emotions, pains, trials, and temptations that we all face as human beings. The only difference was that although He was tempted in all things, just as we are tempted, He did not sin (Heb.4:15). Jesus lived a perfect, sinless life here on earth. This very fact literally qualified Him as the only acceptable sacrifice for us to be forgiven and cleansed from our sin once and for all. In addition, it was fitting for Him to take on humanity so that we could relate to Him for who He really is (His true character and nature). God came to earth as the man, Jesus, so that we might see and understand Him fully. Jesus came so that we could get to know exactly who God is, what He is like, and how He feels about us. The purpose in all of this is so that each one of us might have the opportunity to truly know Him.

No one has ever seen God. But His only Son, who is Himself God, is near to the Father's heart; He has told us about Him —John 1:18, nlt

In my opinion, it is hard for any one of us to relate to

someone who's never had the same experiences we've had or walked in our shoes so to speak. Jesus has done all of that. He has been there and done that! He is the God who understands the human condition and sympathizes with our weaknesses. He is the God who is not far off or far away from us. He is the One who is supreme in nature and yet extremely personable all at the same time. He is the God who truly cares for us and is always in our corner. He is the God who even prays for us without ceasing.

> Therefore He [Jesus] is able, once and forever, to save everyone who comes to God through Him. He lives forever to plead with God on their behalf. —Hebrews 7:25, nlt

There is only one God that exists and this is Him. The One who created you is the true and living God. His name is Jesus.

> That is why we have a great High Priest who has gone to heaven, Jesus the Son of God. Let us cling to Him and never stop trusting Him. This High Priest of ours understands our weaknesses, for He faced all of the same temptations we do, yet He did not sin. So let us come boldly to the throne of our gracious God. There we will receive His mercy, and we will find grace to help us when we need it. —Hebrews 4:14–16, nlt

Telling the Truth #9: Jesus is the Son of God.
Check out the testimony John gave regarding Jesus:

> Then John gave this testimony: "I saw the Spirit come down from heaven as a dove and remain on him. I would not have known him, except that the one who sent me to baptize with water told me, 'The man on

whom you see the Spirit come down and remain is he who will baptize with the Holy Spirit,' I have seen and I testify that this is the Son of God." —John 1:32–34, niv

When it says Jesus is the Son of God, it simply means that Jesus is from God. He is His one and only Son. Now, I can imagine most of you are struggling with this fact, so I will give you some proof that will cause things to make sense for you. The proof is in the real story of the Virgin Mary:

In the sixth month, God sent the angel Gabriel to Nazareth, a town in Galilee, to a virgin pledged to be married to a man named Joseph, a descendant of David. The virgin's name was Mary. The angel went to her and said, "Greetings, you who are highly favored! The Lord is with you." Mary was greatly troubled at his words and wondered what kind of greeting this might be. But the angel said to her, "Do not be afraid, Mary, you have found favor with God. You will be with child and give birth to a son, and you are to give him the name Jesus. He will be great and will be called the Son of the Most High. The Lord God will give him the throne of his father David, and he will reign over the house of Jacob forever; his kingdom will never end." "How will this be," Mary asked the angel, "since I am a virgin?" The angel answered, "The Holy Spirit will come upon you, and the power of the Most High will overshadow you. So the holy one to be born will be called the Son of God. —Luke 1:26–35, niv

Mary was a virgin when she had Jesus. The scripture clearly states what happened. Mary had a miracle impregnation when God's Holy Spirit overshadowed her. God spoke Jesus into Mary just like He spoke and created the oceans, land, day, and night. Mary remained a virgin until after she and Joseph married each other. That is why Jesus (the name given by God) is the Son of God.

Why did God choose Mary?

Why did God choose Mary? Was she extra special? No. Mary was an ordinary girl, a teenager as a matter of fact. God likes to do extraordinary things with regular people who love Him and want Him to use us for His glory! Therefore, God chose Mary as a "vessel" in which to bring His Son into the world for you and me. Although God obviously loved Mary and she was "highly favored," she was never the point or the one to be worshiped. Jesus is the point and the only one we are to worship.

> Long ago God spoke many times and in many ways to our ancestors through the prophets. But now in these final days, He has spoken to us through His Son. God promised everything to the Son as an inheritance, and through the Son He made the universe and everything in it. The Son reflects God's own glory, and everything about Him represents God exactly. He sustains the universe by the mighty power of His command. After He died to cleanse us from the stain of sin, He sat down in the place of honor at the right hand of the majestic God of heaven." —Hebrews 1:1–3, nlt

Telling the Truth #10: Jesus is the Messiah.

According to Jewish history, Israel was under Roman rulership up until the fourth Christian century. The Romans had governmental authority over the Jewish people in their own country. Israel (including its capital, Jerusalem) basically became a Roman province during this time. The Jews believed that the "Messiah," sent by God as His representative, would come and deliver them from the Roman rulership. *Messiah* in Hebrew (the original language of the Old Testament) means, "anointed one." In the Greek language (the original language of the New Testament), Messiah is translated as "Christos" in which we derive the word "Christ" in the English language.

This Messiah was to be a descendant of David (a prominent king of Israel in the Old Testament whom God said was a man after His own heart). It was also said that the Messiah would be a warriorlike conquering king. This king would basically "kick the Romans out" and establish a kingdom without end (lasting forever). As a result of the institution of this kingdom, the Jewish people would be restored to their rightful place to a position of authority in the world.

So in short, the Messiah, or the Christ, was to be their Savior. All the Old Testament prophecies (information spoken about the future before it happened) of the coming Messiah were true. For example, the prophecy that stated that the Messiah was to be a descendant of David (Ps.132:10–11) was fulfilled at the birth of Jesus. The proof is clearly stated in the genealogy of Jesus (Matt. 1:1–17). The genealogy states in Matthew 1:16 that Joseph was the husband of Mary (the woman whom God chose to bring His Son, Jesus, into the world as mentioned before). It also records Joseph as being from the same lineage as David and therefore, making Jesus an actual descendant of David. Likewise, when it comes to the prophecy of the Messiah being a king of an everlasting kingdom, please refer to the songs about Jesus in Chapter 5 of Revelation:

And they sang a new song: "You are worthy to take the scroll and to open its seals, because you were slain, and with your blood you purchased men for God from every tribe and language and people and nation. You have made them to be a kingdom and priests to serve our God, and they will reign on the earth." Then I looked and heard the voice of many angels, numbering thousands upon thousands, and ten thousand times ten thousand. They encircled the throne and the living creatures and the elders. In a loud voice they sang: "Worthy is the Lamb, who was slain, to receive power and wealth and wisdom and strength and honor and glory and praise!" Then I heard every creature in heaven and on earth and under the earth and on the sea, and all that is in them, singing: "To him who sits on the throne and to the Lamb be praise and honor and glory and power, for ever and ever!" —Revelation 5:9–13, niv

The Messiah is the "anointed one" sent by God to be the Savior and Lord of not just the Jews, but also the entire world, to save them from the penalty of their sin, eternal death. Jesus is the Christ, "the Messiah". He is the Savior for you, me and everybody everywhere. Check out what He said to His disciples when He appeared to them after His resurrection:

He said to them, "This is what I told you while I was still with you: Everything must be fulfilled that is written about me in the Law of Moses, the Prophets and the Psalms." Then he opened their minds so they could understand the Scriptures. He told them, "This is what is written: The Christ will suffer and rise from the dead on the third day, and repentance and forgiveness of sins will be preached in his name to all nations, beginning at Jerusalem. —Luke 24: 44–47, niv

Also read what Jesus said to a Samaritan woman during their conversation in the Book of John:

"God is spirit, and his worshipers must worship in spirit and in truth." The woman said, "I know that Messiah" (called Christ) "is coming. When he comes, he will explain everything to us." Then Jesus declared, "I who speak to you am he.'" —John 4:24–26, niv

In addition, let's look at the response of one of Jesus's twelve disciples when Jesus asked them a question about His identity:

When Jesus came to the region of Caesarea Philippi, he asked his disciples, "Who do people say the Son of Man is?" They replied, "Some say John the Baptist;

others say Elijah; and still others, Jeremiah or one of the prophets." "But what about you?" he asked. "Who do you say I am?" Simon Peter answered, "You are the Christ, the Son of the living God." Jesus replied, "Blessed are you, Simon son of Jonah, for this was not revealed to you by man, but by My Father in heaven."
—Matthew 16:13–17, niv

I know I'm giving you proof overkill, but I still welcome you to read the following scriptures that further validate this truth that Jesus is the Messiah:

An Excerpt From Peter's First Sermon

"Men of Israel, listen to this: Jesus of Nazareth was a man accredited by God to you by miracles, wonders and signs, which God did among you through him, as you yourselves know. This man was handed over to you by God's set purpose and foreknowledge; and you, with the help of wicked men, put him to death by nailing him to the cross. But God raised him from the dead, freeing him from the agony of death, because it was impossible for death to keep its hold on him. David said about him: "'I saw the Lord always before me. Because he is at my right hand, I will not be shaken. Therefore my heart is glad and my tongue rejoices; my body also will live in hope, because you will not abandon me to the grave, nor will you let your Holy One see decay. You have made known to me the paths of life; you will fill me with joy in your presence.' "Brothers, I can tell you confidently that the patriarch David died and was buried, and his tomb is here to this day. But he was a prophet and knew that God had promised him on oath that he would place one of his descendants on his throne. Seeing what was ahead, he spoke of the resurrection of the Christ, that he was not abandoned to the grave, nor did his body see decay. God has raised this Jesus to life, and we are all witnesses of the fact. Exalted to the right hand of God, he has received from the Father the promised Holy Spirit and has poured out what you now see and hear. For David did not ascend to heaven, and yet he said, "'The Lord said to my Lord: 'Sit at my right hand until I make your enemies a footstool for your feet.'" "Therefore let all Israel be assured of this: God has made this Jesus, whom you crucified, both Lord and Christ." —Acts 2:22–36, niv

Jesus said to her [Martha], "I am the resurrection and the life. He who believes in me will live, even though he dies; and whoever lives and believes in me will never die. Do you believe this?" "Yes, Lord," she told him, "I believe that you are the Christ, the Son of God, who was to come into the world." —John 11:25–27, niv

Chapter 5

How Can I Be Sure That Jesus Is the Only Way to Be Saved?

Telling the Truth #11: Jesus is the only way to receive eternal life.

Jesus answered, "I am the way and the truth and the life. No one comes to the Father [God] except through me." —John 14:6, niv

Here we see that Jesus says that He is "the way, and the truth, and the life"(referring to eternal life). Notice that Jesus never said that He was one of the many options to know God and have eternal life. In fact, Jesus clearly states that He is the *only way* to know God and have eternal life. Jesus said, "No one comes to the Father [God] except through me" (John 14:6, niv). In addition, note that Jesus does not say, "I am one of the truths, or one of the many truths along the path leading to God." This is very important because in today's culture, you have received a different message. The message of today reads, "You can choose whatever truth you prefer because they all lead to the same God!" Although this sounds good, God completely disagrees with this message. Jesus said, "I am the way and *the truth*" (John 14:6, niv, emphasis added). This statement made by Jesus, means that He is the *only truth* that exists when it comes to knowing God. As a result, it dispels any other way to know God, outside of coming to Jesus. Jesus is not one of the many choices on a "drive-thru dollar menu" of religion where you get salvation at the pickup window. He is the only choice to receive salvation.

Many of you have asked the question, "I see all these different religions out here, but which one is the truth?" You might have even thought to yourself, "What is truth? I just want to know the truth." The answer to what you are searching for is Jesus. Jesus is the truth. He is not a truth among many truths, but He is the *only truth* there is. When you find Jesus, you find the truth and this truth will give you a life of freedom:

> To the Jews who had believed him, Jesus said, "If you hold to my teaching, you are really my disciples. Then you will know the truth, and the truth will set you free." —John 8:31–32, niv

> "Now this is eternal life: that they may know you, the only true God, and Jesus Christ, whom You have sent." —John 17:3, niv

Jesus makes it clear that knowing Him means that we live our lives in accordance with His teaching (aka the Word or the Bible). He also points out that knowing Him in relationship means you have eternal life. Therefore, one of the greatest facts about knowing Jesus (the truth) is that He sets you free from the bondage and penalty of sin in exchange for a life of real freedom and salvation (which includes eternal life). He can set you free from whatever has you bound and whatever pain you are experiencing emotionally and physically. Maybe you're like me and you've had a troubled childhood. Maybe the abuse you've encountered from your past is causing some character issues and problems for you now in your adulthood. You might even feel trapped because you don't know the answer to the problems or how to get free. Trust me when I tell you, I know how you feel and Jesus is the only answer. He can set you free from any struggle or addiction you are experiencing, no matter what it is. To know Jesus is to know true freedom. Jesus said in His word that He came to set the captives free (Isa. 61:1). Please understand that the freedom that you experience with knowing Jesus (the truth) covers all aspects of your life, including knowing the truth about various religions. In other words, this "truth" can set you free from the lies of all the false religions that deny Jesus as the only way to know God and have eternal life.

Jesus, please save my Muslim friends!

This really hits home for me as I think about a good friend I had in college who happened to be a Muslim. He was the type of guy who would give the very shirt off of his back for you. He was really one of the nicest people you would ever want to meet. He and I attended the same economics class and even studied together. Although we had just met during my last year at the university, we were very cool and spent a considerable amount of time together. During the second semester of that particular year, I had an assignment from my international cultures class that involved researching a religion that I was not familiar with. My professor wanted me to pick a religion outside my faith so I could be exposed to different cultures. This was actually the purpose of the class, learning about different cultures. Therefore, I shared my research project with my Muslim friend and asked for his help. He agreed to help me and took me to his mosque so I could observe their service and interview the leaders as a part of my research.

The mosque was within walking distance from the school and when I got there, I recall seeing all different races. During the service, the leader began talking to everyone about doing good to others and maintaining peace. As he continued to share, I thought to myself, "Man, this sounds OK and it's very similar to the Christian teaching in a lot of ways." For the first time, I could see for my own eyes how deceptive this "faith" really was. The Muslim teacher did not mention anything that you could pinpoint as something morally wrong. After the service, I met with one of the leaders and conducted an interview to gather the information that I needed for my assignment. When I was finished with the interview questions for my paper, I began to ask some other questions about how they viewed and felt about Jesus. Our conversation about Jesus was very interesting and it is one that I will never forget. It was like everything lined up to what I knew about Christianity until we started talking about Jesus.

I call this the "Jesus Factor" because it truly divides people (as mentioned in Chapter 1). The Muslim leader stated that he believed that Jesus existed and that He was a great prophet and teacher, who eventually died, end of story. He denied that Jesus was the Son of God, the way to receive eternal life, and that He resurrected from the dead. I walked out of that mosque with my heart breaking for my Muslim friends because I knew that they were only following what they thought to be the truth. I mean, many of them had been raised as Muslims from birth, never knowing that Jesus is the truth that they had always been searching for. I questioned God that day and wondered, "How in the world could these nice people be on a one-way ticket to hell?" As I walked back to the university, I prayed that God would lift the deception and save my Muslim friends. I prayed that the words of truth that I spoke about Jesus would penetrate their hearts. I prayed that though they were "blind," their eyes would be opened so that they could see the truth (Jesus).

To be real about it, I could not bear the thought of them dying without Christ and going to hell. It hurt me so badly to even think about it and caused my eyes to well up with tears. The good news is that God loved them even more than I did, and that's why He sent His Son, Jesus Christ. During that walk back to the school, I also came to a whole new sense of responsibility for people like me who know the truth (Jesus). With a heavy burden for my Muslim friend, I realized that we (Christians) are to stop holding back. We are to share the truth in love because someone else's life is literally depending on it! That is why I am sharing the truth with you today. Again, Jesus is the truth! Receive Him and you have the truth.

Now, I want us to look at John 14:6 again. Let's focus on the part where Jesus says He is, "the life."

Jesus answered, "I am the way and the truth and the life. No one comes to the Father [God] except through Me." —John 14:6, niv

When it comes to eternal life, Jesus tells us that He is it! I want you to think about it this way. Let's say for example you're riding in a car on your way to your favorite amusement park. When you get close to the amusement park, you begin to see signs that indicate which direction to go or which exit you need to take to get to the park. If you want to arrive at the park and enjoy the rides, food, and fun, you must accept the right way to get there. You can say, "Well I don't believe that this is the right exit or direction," but it won't matter. You must follow the specific directions or you will be lost. The same is true when it comes to salvation. Jesus is the only way to get to the destination of eternal life. If you choose to not believe it and try to go your own way or another way, you will be lost. To be lost means that you don't have the truth and therefore, you don't have eternal life. All those who accept Jesus are saved and all those who don't are lost:

For the Son of Man has come to save that which was lost. —Matthew 18:11

Salvation is found in no one else, for there is no other name under heaven given to men by which we must be saved. —Acts 4:12, niv

So, how do I know if my religion is the truth?
Dear friends, do not believe every spirit, but test the spirits to see whether they are from God, because many false prophets have gone out into the world. This is how you can recognize the Spirit of God: Every spirit that acknowledges that Jesus Christ has come in the flesh is from God, but every spirit that does not

acknowledge Jesus is not from God. This is the spirit of the antichrist, which you have heard is coming and even now is already in the world. –1 John 4:1–3, niv

There are so many different religions out there that it just gets down right confusing. I mean, especially when you don't know what you should be looking for. To help you distinguish the truth from all the false religions that exist in our world today, let's break it down into what I call the "Truth Test." The Truth Test is the test that you can use to see if the church or religion you are a part of is the real deal or simply put, "The Truth."

The Truth Test (It Must)

Acknowledge and teach that Jesus is the Son of God who came to earth as a man, died on the cross, and was resurrected (raised from the dead) so that you could be forgiven of your sins, have an intimate relationship with God (reconciliation), and therefore, have eternal life.

Believe that Jesus was born to a virgin (Virgin Birth), that forgiveness of sin is through Him alone and not through a person in the church (Jesus is the only mediator for our sins), and that He is the only way to receive eternal life.

Believe that the Bible is the *infallible* (certain, reliable) truth of God's divine Word and the *absolute standard* (complete authority) by which we are to live our lives.

Number 1 and 2 of the Truth Test are pretty self-explanatory, but let's talk about number 3 for a minute. The Merriam-Webster Online Dictionary defines *infallible* as "incapable of error; unerring." It also describes this word *infallible* as "incapable of error in defining doctrines touching faith and morals." So the truth here is that the Bible is incapable of error. That means that there are no mistakes in the Bible. None, no not one! It is the hard-core truth and nothing but the truth! In addition, the Bible is the *absolute standard* by which we are to live our lives. That word *absolute* is defined as being "free from imperfection; perfect" (*Merriam-Webster Online Dictionary*). And I want you to note that when something is perfect, that also means that it is complete. Nothing needs to be added to it and nothing needs to be taken away from it. Basically, just leave it alone; it's perfect! Therefore, the Bible is the perfect and complete standard or what I call the "bench mark" of authority for you, me, and everybody everywhere.

These facts about the Bible are very important because there are tons of religions that offer other books as their basis for truth. In fact, there are even some religions, claiming to be Christian, that require you to read their supplemental pamphlets and books in addition to the Bible. I'm sorry if these statements will step on some toes, but remember ya'll, I'm telling the truth! Check out what God has to say about adding or subtracting anything from His Word (the Bible):

> You shall not add to the word which I am commanding you, nor take away from it, that you may keep the commandments of the LORD your God which I command you. —Deuteronomy 4:2

> Every word of God is flawless; he is a shield to those who take refuge in him. Do not add to his words, or he will rebuke you and prove you a liar. —Proverbs 30:5–6, niv

> Every word of God proves true. He is a shield to all who come to him for protection. Do not add to his words, or he may rebuke you and expose you as a liar. He defends all who come to Him for protection. —Proverbs 30:5–6, nlt

> I warn everyone who hears the words of the prophecy of this book: If anyone adds anything to them, God will add to him the plagues described in this book. And if anyone takes words away from this book of prophecy, God will take away from him his share in

the tree of life and in the holy city, which are described in this book. He who testifies to these things says, "Yes, I am coming soon." Amen. Come, Lord Jesus. The grace of the Lord Jesus be with God's people. Amen. –Revelation 22:18–21, niv

What about the different religions within the Christian church? How do I know which one is the truth or the right one to go to?

The answer to this question is the same as above. If the church that you attend does not pass the Truth Test, then it is not the right place for you or anybody else. You see, what we might call different religions within the Christian faith are mostly different denominations. For example, you have a wide range of denominations, such as, the Baptist, Charismatic, nondenominational, Assembly of God, Pentecostal, Church of God in Christ and the list goes on and on. Now, there are a few exceptions, such as, the existence of "Christian" cults, which are religions that parade under the Christian name, but in reality they have abandoned the truth for a lie. These cults fail the Truth Test every time because their core beliefs deviate from accurate biblical teaching. These religions are the worst of their kind because they are crafty in taking scripture completely out of context to perpetuate their error. Many of these cults are very controlling and discourage you from interacting with any family or friends who don't attend their church. These cults believe that they are the only "true church." It is their belief that the real Christians that actually interpret scripture in its proper context are the ones who have it wrong. Beware of these cults and ask Jesus (the truth) to guide you clear away from their deceptive grasp.

Why are there so many different denominations within the Christian faith?

The truth is that the early church of Christians or believers were just one church (aka the body of believers). To show you the history behind the birth of each denomination within today's Christian community would literally take another book or volumes upon volumes of books just to explain. The reason is because there is tons of church history that outlines the birth and progression of different denominations. However, this history can be summarized into one major contributing factor called, Church Reformation. *Reformation* is defined as "advocating change; to correct or improve" (*The New International Webster's Standard Dictionary* 2006 Edition). The need for church reformation existed because the church as a whole got away from the foundational truths of Christianity. Reformation became essential throughout church history as man-made traditions, preferences, and rules that deviated from the Bible (Scriptures) institutionalized the church. And guess what? That goes completely against what we talked about in number 3 of our Truth Test, to believe that the Bible is the infallible truth of God's divine Word and the absolute standard by which we are to live our lives.

These campaigns of reformation were sparked by believers who received revelation into the scriptures from the Holy Spirit (God's Spirit in us). Revelation is to finally see the truth that was always staring you dead in the face. Revelation communicates the truths of God's Word regarding His desires and plan for us in our relationship with Him, even after I get saved. These truths include everything Jesus died and rose for us to have. That includes salvation and so much more! These biblical truths challenge religious thinking because they can only be comprehended or understood by the Holy Spirit. I define religious thinking as man-made ideas, rules and regulations about God but not from God. When you connect with God in relationship, the opposite of religion, you have His Spirit in you and you receive the truth that is from Him. God's Holy Spirit inside you gives witness or testifies that this revelation you hear and see is truth.

In addition, the Reformation movements often brought about revivals. Reformation and revivals kind of go hand in hand. Here's the thing, God desires none to be lost and all to be saved (1 Tim. 2:4). Therefore, He uses people to express this love of His gospel as demonstrated in His Son, Jesus Christ. In several cases throughout history, this has been done in powerful ways where God has poured out His Spirit on thousands of people all at the same time and great miracles, signs, and wonders are experienced. These moves of God are called revivals.

These revivals have brought about revolutions in church history while never compromising the truth about God and His Son, Jesus Christ. In fact, any revival from God has always been founded on the truth of God's love in the gospel of Jesus Christ. However, many people in the church have rejected these revivals because they did not understand or recognize them as new moves of God. The truth is that we often reject and criticize what we don't understand.

The reformations and revivals that were birthed from the heart of God were essentially led by people trying to encourage everyone (including the church) to accept the true and living God, Jesus Christ, in all of His deity. These reformists tried to revive the people back to their early roots of Christianity as one body of believers exemplifying a lifestyle founded on biblical principles. However, it seems that the very thing these individuals didn't want to see, the church separating into different denominations, kept happening as a result of their efforts. In fact, history shows that this kept happening inadvertently. My definition of *inadvertently* is when something happens by accident that you didn't plan to happen at all. It just happens even though that wasn't what you were trying for. Sometimes it can be good and other times it can be bad. So anyway, the groups of people that accepted the reforms eventually became denominations within themselves. And the fact of the matter is that this just kept on happening over and over again like a boomerang being thrown out there for one purpose and returning to hit you in the head with things you didn't expect.

The long and short of it is that whatever denomination

you choose is fine as long as they teach and practice what I mentioned in the Truth Test. Some people like to worship God loudly and others like to do it quietly. Some prefer fiery enthusiastic preaching and others like to hear messages in a monotone, even kilt voice. Some people like to stand up and lift their hands when they praise God and others prefer to remain seated.

So although many people have different preferences of the type of church they like better, it's all the same if they have the same faith in Jesus Christ. Remember that Jesus said in John 14:6 that no one can come to the Father (God) except through Him. That tells us that no matter the denomination, all who know Jesus, know God and are a part of one big, humungous family called the church.

Jesus is coming back, are you ready?

Jesus died, was buried, and was resurrected for us. And guess what? He's coming back to make good on His promise of eternal life for all who know Him (have a relationship). Here's how it's going down. All those who have already died before His return will be raised up (resurrected) first and then those who are alive at His coming will follow:

> And now, brothers and sisters, I want you to know what will happen to the Christians who have died so you will not be full of sorrow like people who have no hope. For since we believe that Jesus died and was raised to life again, we also believe that when Jesus comes, God will bring back with Jesus all the Christians who have died. I can tell you this directly from the Lord: We who are still living when the Lord returns will not rise to meet Him ahead of those who are in their graves. For the Lord Himself will come down from heaven with a commanding shout, with the call of the archangel, and with the trumpet call of God. First, all the Christians who have died will rise

from their graves. Then, together with them, we who are still alive and remain on the earth will be caught up in the clouds to meet the Lord in the air and remain with Him forever. —1 Thessalonians 4:13–17, nlt

The only thing about this is that no one knows when Jesus will return; therefore, you have to be ready! His return will happen when you least expect it. The Bible compares it to a thief in the night:

I really don't need to write to you about how and when all this will happen, dear brothers and sisters. For you know quite well that the day of the Lord will come unexpectedly, like a thief in the night. When people are saying, "All is well; everything is peaceful and secure," then disaster will fall upon them as suddenly as a woman's birth pains begin when her child is about to be born. And there will be no escape. –1 Thessalonians 5:1–3, nlt

I hear all of that, but people have been saying Jesus is coming back for decades and He hasn't come. Some people have gone so far as to predict a date and that day came and went, and still no Jesus. How can this be? Let me answer this question by simply clarifying two important facts. First, Jesus said Himself that nobody knows the day or the hour of His return. And the last time I checked, "nobody" means nobody, not a single person. Check out the following account of this statement:

However, no one knows the day or the hour when these things will happen, not even the angels in heaven or the Son himself. Only the Father knows. When the Son of Man (Jesus) returns, it will be like it was in Noah's day. In those days before the flood, the people were enjoying banquets and parties and weddings right up to the time Noah entered the boat. People didn't

realize what was going to happen until the flood came and swept them all away. That is the way it will be when the Son of Man comes. Two men will be working together in the field; one will be taken, the other left. Two women will be grinding flour at the mill; one will be taken, the other left. So be prepared, because you don't know what day your Lord is coming. Know this: A homeowner who knew exactly when a burglar was coming would stay alert and not permit the house to be broken into. You also must be ready all the time. For the Son of Man will come when least expected.
—Matthew 24:36–44, nlt

Secondly, God is not taking a long time as we might think. For Him, it's not even like that. The truth is that He is being patient so that all might come to know Him and be saved. I mean, when we really think about it, God is showing us yet again how much He truly loves us. He's waiting, trying to give those of us who have not accepted His love chance after chance after chance! Remember that I mentioned earlier that God desires none to be lost, but all to be saved (1 Tim. 2:4).

First, I want to remind you that in the last days there will be scoffers who will laugh at the truth and do every evil thing they desire. This will be their argument: 'Jesus promised to come back, did He? Then where is He? Why, as far back as anyone can remember, everything has remained exactly the same since the world was first created. They deliberately forget that God made the heavens by the word of His command, and He brought the earth up from the water and surrounded it with water. Then He used the water to destroy the world with a mighty flood. And God has also commanded that the heavens and the earth will be consumed by fire on the day of judgment, when ungodly people will perish. But you must not forget, dear friends, that a day is like a thousand years to the

Lord, and a thousand years is like a day. The Lord isn't really being slow about His promise to return, as some people think. No, He is being patient for your sake. He does not want anyone to perish, so He is giving more time for everyone to repent. –2 Peter 3:3–9, nlt

Now even though God's mercies are new every morning and His patience is enduring. Make no mistake, this window of time will not last forever. I urge you to get ready for His coming. Anyone who dies knowing Him doesn't have to sweat anything. That means that if your grandmother died knowing Jesus, you might be sad in the context of the loss you feel, but you don't have to feel forever saddened in the context of her life. Her life is hidden in Christ forever. There is no end to the story of her life. She lives on with Jesus. Therefore, you are not without hope. That's why the Bible encourages us that we don't have to feel hopeless and depressed about the Christians who have died because we know that there is life after death for the believer (1 Thess. 4:13). Once again, Jesus is coming back, are you ready?

Chapter 6

How Can I Be Saved and Receive This Free Gift of Eternal Life?

In sharing the truth to this question, I want us to look at a true Bible event in Acts Chapter 16. This true story is a "question and answer" (Q&A) session between a jailer and Paul and Silas, servants of God.

Here's the scene. Paul and Silas were severely beaten and unjustly thrown into prison for preaching the gospel. Yes the gospel, the good news of God's love for you and the entire world. The same truth I've been sharing with you. The interesting thing about it is that what sparked the whole arrest was when Paul cast out an evil spirit of divination from a fortune-teller slave girl. When the slave girl's owners realized that they weren't going to be able to make any money off of her fortune-telling, they got extremely angry and dragged Paul and Silas to the local authorities (Acts 16:19–21). I mean this was their business and the girl was their moneymaker. Today this practice is the whole psychic circuit, the psychic phone lines, places you go to get "readings," and even television shows that make it seem OK while others prey on people who have lost their love ones. Anyway, Paul and Silas were placed in chains and put in the maximum-security area of the prison (Acts 16:23–24).

At about midnight, Paul and Silas were praying and singing praises to God when all of a sudden, an earthquake hit. It was so great that it shook the foundations of the prison house and miraculously all of the prison doors were opened and all of the prisoners' chains were unfastened (Acts 16:25–

26). When the warden saw the prison doors opened, he almost committed suicide because he thought all the prisoners had escaped (Acts 16:27). In those days, the jailer could suffer serious consequences if a prisoner escaped. That's why he was about to kill himself.

OK, now let's pick it up in verse 28 where the Q&A session is about to begin and where the warden gets ready to make what I call "his life's decision."

> But Paul shouted, "Don't harm yourself! We are all here!" The jailer called for lights, rushed in and fell trembling before Paul and Silas. He then brought them out and asked, "Sirs, what must I do to be saved?" They replied, "Believe in the Lord Jesus, and you will be saved—you and your household." Then they spoke the word of the Lord to him and to all the others in his house. At that hour of the night the jailer took them and washed their wounds; then immediately he and all his family were baptized. The jailer brought them into his house and set a meal before them; he was filled with joy because he had come to believe in God—he and his whole family. —Acts 16: 28–34, niv

Telling the Truth #12: All I have to do to be saved and receive eternal life is believe in Jesus.

> "For God so loved the world that he gave his one and only Son, that whoever believes in him shall not perish but have eternal life. For God did not send his Son into the world to condemn the world, but to save the world through him. Whoever believes in him is not condemned, but whoever does not believe stands condemned already because he has not believed in the name of God's one and only Son." —John 3:16–18, niv

That's it; that's all you have to do. It's that simple. The "one stop shop" to salvation is to *believe*. You see God doesn't make it hard. His plan of salvation for you is so easy that even a child can understand it and receive Jesus. And let me tell you. In my time serving as a children's pastor, I've been fortunate to see it. I've seen many children hear the message of God's love for them and respond by believing in Jesus with all of their hearts.

What does it mean to believe?

To believe in Jesus means that I put my faith and trust in Him. It means that I accept Jesus as God as well as what He's done for me. When I talk about believing what He has done for me (us), I'm simply referring to what this book is all about, the gospel (the good news). This is God's love for you in action (as I mentioned earlier). Jesus paid the price for the penalty of sin for you and me through His death on the cross and then was resurrected by His own power so that we could be reconciled back to God in relationship. As a result of Jesus resurrection, we too can be raised up when we die into eternal life if we just believe.

The moment I truly believe in Jesus is the exact same moment I receive Him. I'm talking about relationship. It's all about relationship. Believing in Jesus is receiving Jesus and receiving Jesus is accepting Him in relationship.

> All that the Father gives me will come to me, and whoever comes to me I will never drive away. —John 6:37, niv

Jesus wants to be your best friend! No matter who you are, what you have or haven't done, what you have or haven't accomplished, it really doesn't matter. What matters most is that you can never know who you really are until you get connected to the one who created you. You can't be truly fulfilled as a person and live out your real purpose in life until you get to know God. God is the real true and living God. He is your maker, your creator:

> Know that the LORD Himself is God; It is He who made us, and not we ourselves; We are His people and the sheep of His pasture. —Psalm 100:3

And guess what? He has a name. His name is Jesus!

I'm forgiven!

When I truly believe the gospel, I am no longer blind but I can see—my reality for what it really is. And that reality is that I'm a sinner who needs to be saved from the penalty of my sins (like everyone else). I also realize that Jesus is the one and only Savior who is able to save me. Therefore, I automatically repent. To repent means to turn from my sin and turn to God. That's the act of repentance. I'm basically saying, "Jesus, I recognize that I'm a sinner. So, I now embrace Your forgiveness for me and turn from my old life of living without You." You see because of the price Jesus paid, you can know without a shadow of doubt that you're forgiven of all sin. By the way, that includes your past, present, and future sins. You literally stand in a continual state of "I'm forgiven." All you have to do now is receive His forgiveness.

Check this out. The Bible says that if we confess our sins, God is faithful and just to forgive us of our sins and cleanse (purify) us from all unrighteousness (1 John 1:9). This is like taking a shower with a soap that will keep you clean forever and you never have to "sweat" getting dirty again. That is what the blood of Jesus has done for us. It has cleansed us from all sin. Yeah, you might fall down into sin and "get dirty," but you can get back up again. How? The reason is because the blood of Jesus keeps you clean. Therefore, you remain forgiven. The Bible also says that God remembers our sin no more. He literally blots them out (Isa. 43:25). God says that as far as the east is from the west is as far as He has removed your sins away from you (Ps. 103:12).

If you've never received the ultimate forgiveness of God (demonstrated through His Son Jesus Christ), I encourage you right now in this very moment to do so. That's it. Receive His forgiveness. It's been waiting for you all along. You might ask, "What if I've received His forgiveness before, but I've walked away from God, I have back slidden?" If that's you, I also encourage you to receive His forgiveness. God's forgiveness has never left you; it's still there for you. It's OK, you can get back on track today. Yes, you just receive it. His forgiveness is right there for you. All of you say this with me, "I am forgiven!" Say it with me one more time and feel free to scream it at the top of your lungs if you want to: "I am forgiven. Yes, I'm forgiven because Jesus loves me!"

Life without Jesus is empty.

My heart goes out to all of you out there because I know that you have been searching and searching, trying to fill your emptiness with everything you think will meet your deepest need. The only thing is that there is nothing in this world that can truly meet the need you are trying to fulfill. In other words, nothing and no one can take the place of God in your life. That's why drugs, sex, money, success, friends, relationships, you name it, is still not doing it for you! You see, God made you with a need for Him that *only* He Himself can fulfill. That longing and place in your heart was meant for Him. God is the only one who can complete you. I'll say it again, please hear me with all of your heart. God is the only one who can complete you. Therefore, whoever you are, without God, you are totally incomplete.

Many of you have realized that there is something missing in your life. Maybe you've never been able to really put your finger on what that something is until now. You have thought to yourself, "There has got to be more to life than what I'm experiencing!" Some of you have asked questions such as, "Why am I here?" "What is life really all about?" Jesus is the answer to these questions. In fact, your very purpose, reason for being, in life is to enjoy a loving, close, and intimate relationship with God through His Son, Jesus Christ, and share it with the world. God loves you so much and all He wants is to be your best friend. I'm not talking about religion or just going to church; I'm talking about relationship. It's all about relationship. All you have to do to start this relationship is to receive Jesus into your life by simply asking Him. "Yes, it's that simple. All you have to do is ask! Jesus loves you so much and He is only one ask away." Check out what God says in the Book of Romans:

> If you confess with your mouth, "Jesus is Lord," and believe in your heart that God raised him from the dead, you will be saved. —Romans 10:9, niv

You see, when you confess Jesus as Lord, you are acknowledging Him as your Savior (the Messiah or Savior of the world as mentioned earlier). You were drowning in your sin, but now you've chosen to accept the "life preserver" of salvation God has thrown to you. You wave the hand of your heart saying, "Here I am, Lord. Save me!" So now, Jesus is not just the Savior of the whole world, but He becomes the one (that life preserver) who has now saved you. He is now your very own, personal Savior! Confessing Jesus as Lord is also saying, "God you're in charge of my life. You're in charge of all my decisions in life. You're in charge of everything concerning me and about me. I'm yours, Lord." Therefore, confessing Jesus as Lord is verbally expressing, from your heart, your acknowledgement of Him as the one and only Savior and your decision to surrender yourself and your life to Him.

That does not mean that you try to clean yourself up before you come to God. Many of you have said, "I respect God too much and I will come to Him later in my life. When I'm ready to settle down and live right, then I will come to Him." First, living a lifestyle of relationship with God is not boring. It's the freest life that exists. Secondly, you can't clean yourself up no matter how hard you try. Jesus took care of the being perfect and absolutely righteous part for you. All you have to do is accept that fact and walk with Him in relationship as He fixes the broken pieces of your life. He wants all of you and that includes your mess. Surrender yourself and your mess to Him, He can handle it! In fact, His loving arms are open wide to you right now. He's not mad at you. He loves you. Let Him love you. That's it, let Him love you because He already does so very much.

I believe the gospel and want to receive Jesus.

If that's you and you believe this gospel and want to receive Jesus into your heart and into your life right now, I invite you to pray this prayer with me:

Jesus, I recognize that I'm a sinner and You love me so much that you gave Your very life for me. Jesus, I repent of all my sin and receive Your forgiveness. Thank you for Your forgiveness Jesus. Jesus, I believe the whole truth about You. I know that Your gospel is the truth. I believe that you died on the cross and that you were resurrected by Your own power, so I too, could be resurrected into a new life with you. I confess you as Lord right now, Jesus. Take full control of my life. I surrender myself to You. Come into my heart right now, Lord, save me. I receive Your love and want You to be my best friend as we enjoy an awesome relationship together from this day forward and forever. Amen.

Wow! Guess what? You just made the biggest decision you will ever make for your life! If Jesus were to come back this very instant, you would go straight to heaven! Each and every one of you who prayed that prayer is saved! When it's time for you to leave this earth, you will spend eternity with God forever! You now have eternal life! It's God's free gift to you and no one can take it away! In fact, there is a huge party going on in heaven at this very moment all because of you and the decision that you have made (Luke 15:7). You don't have to be afraid anymore when you go to sleep, feeling uncertain about life after death. It's been settled. You have been reconciled with God through His Son, Jesus Christ, and therefore, He is now your best friend! Yes, congratulations my friends, you are saved!

And let me tell you, it doesn't just stop there. God has an awesome plan and purpose for your life. The Bible says in the Book of Jeremiah that before you were even a growing baby in your mother's belly, God knew you (Jer. 1:5). He also already has great plans for your life (Jer. 29:11). Just as I was before Christ, you were disconnected from God on that road of death and destruction. But now, you are tight with Him, connected, on this amazing path of new life and all its fullness in Christ. And now that you are connected to Him, you are therefore also plugged into His purpose for your life!

Jesus has now taken your entire past. Your past mistakes, failures, you name it—no matter how bad. Your past way of living was a lie in which you were being somebody you were never born to be. Many of you tried to be someone you weren't just to fit in because you were trapped by insecurity. It's all over now! You can finally give the biggest exhale of your life in the sigh of the relief you've been longing for. The relief of being set free from the bondage of sin. The burden has been lifted and taken by Jesus. All of your pain, all of your hurt, all of your mess, all of your baggage, everything has been lifted and taken by Jesus. It doesn't matter. He loves you for you and He wants it all! It's like this. You can give Him every single skeleton in your closet without being judged and still be backed 100 percent by His unconditional love. No judging, just loving! I know you have been tired of being tired, but you can now relax for good and rest in Him. In Him alone you have true rest for your soul.

> Then Jesus said, "Come to me, all of you who are weary and carry heavy burdens, and I will give you rest. Take

my yoke upon you. Let me teach you, because I am humble and gentle at heart, and you will find rest for your souls." —Matthew 11:28–29, nlt

I pray right now for total healing from the emotional scars from your past and the hurtful, negative words that have been spoken over you. In the name of Jesus, I cancel these word curses off of your life and declare the healing power and restoration of Jesus to your mind, body, and soul. I now call forth God's divine plan for you and declare this plan to take root in your life right now, from this day forward. No matter what you have been told about yourself, let me tell you the truth. You are special, unique, extremely important, and valuable beyond comparison. And I do mean beyond comparison! You are God's best, created by Him and for Him. He has and will always love you with an everlasting love as your perfect everlasting Father.

Receive the Holy Spirit.

As for me [John the Baptist], I baptize you with water for repentance, but He [Jesus] who is coming after me is mightier than I, and I am not fit to remove His sandals; *He will baptize you with the Holy Spirit* and fire. —Matthew 3:11, emphasis added

But *the Helper, the Holy Spirit*, whom the Father will send in My [Jesus's] name, He will teach you all things, and bring to your remembrance all that I said to you. —John 14:26, emphasis added

"In one of these meetings as He [Jesus] was eating a meal with them (the disciples), He told them, 'Do not leave Jerusalem until the Father sends you what He promised. Remember, I have told you about this before. John baptized with water, but in just a few days *you will be baptized with the Holy Spirit.'"... "But when the Holy Spirit has come upon you, you will receive power and will tell people about Me everywhere—in* Jerusalem, throughout Judea, in Samaria, and to the ends of the earth." —Acts 1:4–5, 8, nlt, emphasis added

While Apollos was at Corinth, Paul took the road through the interior and arrived at Ephesus. There he found some disciples and asked them, *"Did you receive the Holy Spirit when you believed?" They answered, "No, we have not even heard that there is a Holy Spirit."* Paul asked, "Then what baptism did you receive?" "John's baptism," they replied. Paul said, "John's baptism was a baptism of repentance. He told the people to believe in the one coming after him, that is, in Jesus." On hearing this, they were baptized into the name of the Lord Jesus. When Paul placed his hands on them, the Holy Spirit came on them, and they spoke in tongues and prophesied. There were about twelve men in all. –Acts 19:1–7, niv, emphasis added

The Holy Spirit is God's Spirit inside of you. The Holy Spirit is our helper, Counselor, protector, and Comforter. He teaches us things about God that we could not know on our own. He gives us the power we need to witness (tell others about Jesus) for Him. And check this out; the power of the Holy Spirit in us also helps us live for Jesus when everything in this world is trying to pull us the other direction. He is all of this and so much more! He is literally God living on the inside of you! Jesus promised the Holy Spirit for every believer. He promised that He would baptize us with the Holy Spirit. All we have to do is ask and receive. Let's pray. *Father, You promised the Holy Spirit for every believer. I now pray that each one who has accepted You, Jesus, would now receive Your Holy Spirit. Receive now the Holy Spirit. Amen.*

Now that you are saved, I want to encourage you to do three things:

1. Pray

Prayer is simply talking to God and letting Him speak back to you. It is simply having a conversation with Jesus. You can tell Him everything. Pour out your heart to Him. Spill your guts! It's all good. He is your best friend now and wants to hear everything. Go ahead; hang out with Jesus! By the way, there is no special place or position to pray. I like to have alone prayer times in my room just sitting, on my knees, or flat on my face. Other times, it's in my car while I'm driving. I pray everywhere because God is always there. You can pray to God in your mind on the bus on your way to school. It doesn't matter. You can pray at anytime. It's like logging onto your own private chat room with God that's always at your fingertips. Whenever you want to talk to Him is a good time to pray. And let me tell you, the more you do it, the more you get to know how amazing He is and the closer you become in your relationship.

2. Read the Bible

Check this out! Let me ask you a quick question? Before you play a board game like chess or Monopoly, what is the first thing you have to do to know how to play the game? Some of you got it, that's it! The answer is that you first have to read the directions. We were all created by God (Ps. 100:3) and we too come with directions. Although the Bible is not a bunch of rules and regulations, it is God's Word to you, me, and everybody everywhere that provides direction and real answers for everyday life. God has something to say about your current situation no matter what it is. His daily, weekly, monthly, and yearly "planner" for your life is embodied in it. The Bible is full of truths that when applied, practiced, or what I call "lived out," will literally change your life. This is so important because it is one of the vital keys to growing in your relationship with God, spiritual growth. Now I know that this term *spiritual growth* has confused many of you in the past because you've heard some complicated or downright weird definitions. Therefore, let me clear up some things for you. Spiritual growth is simply growing in your relationship with God. That's it. That is the calm, easy and plain true definition. It's that simple. And since we have already established that Jesus is God, you could really say it like this: "Practicing the Bible helps me grow in my relationship with Jesus." It will help me experience the fullness of the awesome life I now have in Christ. God's desire for every believer is to continuously be growing in their relationships with Him.

The Word of God is no joke! It is living, active and sharper than the sharpest knife, cutting deep into our innermost thoughts and desires (Heb. 4:12). When you read it, it's like God is speaking directly to your heart. He shares Himself and His mind with us by His Word. If I want the mind of Christ, His attitude, how He thinks, His heart, all I have to do is meditate on His Word and it becomes my thinking. The Word literally transforms me by renewing my mind. That is how powerful and living it really is. This Word has even changed how I think about myself and relate to God. For example, I didn't overcome insecurity only by praying. I overcame it by seeing myself the way God sees me, all from reading His Word. When I have needed God's advice on something, He has often provided me with the wisdom I needed through His Word. There have been countless times when I just picked it up and read something that I personally needed to hear for whatever I was experiencing at the time. It is a book for all times. I mean even though the book is old, it never "gets old" if you know what I mean. There is always something new and exciting to learn. God speaks to me all of the time through His Word. In fact, if you want to hear from God, just pick up His Word. I have learned about His true character and grown so close and intimate with Him just by reading and meditating on the Bible. I could go on and on about God's Word, that's how awesome it is! But the key is that practicing it is a vital part of growing in your relationship with Him (James 1:22–25). And you can't live out what you don't know. And you can't know it, if you don't read it. Therefore, dive into it and enjoy the great adventure you will experience in Jesus. You will be glad that you did.

3. Go to Church

Now here's the question, "Why do I go to church?" I mean, why is it important to attend church? In a nutshell, it all boils down to this. The reason I go to church is to grow in my daily relationship with God (aka my walk with Jesus). That is the long and short of it. That's what it's all about. Going to church will help you grow in your relationship with God in the following ways:

Receiving sound biblical teaching: Teaches you how to live your everyday life according to the Bible. This includes learning how to apply the Word in specific situations and challenges you face in life as a believer. Learning to experience God's best for you in every area of your life.

Fellowship: My definition of *fellowship* is basically hanging with the right crew. I mean, you are who you hang around. If you hang out with other Christians who are sold out for God, then it's highly likely that you will stay on that path as well. It is important to surround yourself with the right people. The Bible says, "Bad company corrupts good character" (1 Cor.15:33, niv). Character represents the decisions you make that become your habits. Therefore, if I practice making good decisions, I am developing good character. And if I practice making bad decisions, I am developing bad character. So it is safe to say that good company helps produce good character.

Discipleship: Discipleship comes from the root word, *disciple*, which means follower of Christ. That's what you and I are once we have received Him. And when we read Jesus's mission statement for us as believers at the end of Matthew 28, it says to go into all the world and make disciples. So this tells us that Jesus just doesn't want to see people get saved, end of story, go home and eat a sandwich! No! He wants them saved and then He wants follow-up or follow-through of people being discipled. This takes place through relationships whether in small groups (sometimes home church groups), pastoral and mentor relationships or just basic friendships. In these disciple relationships, someone or a group of people are pouring into your life spiritually with godly advice, prayer, support, and just being a true friend. They are not doing so out of duty, but out of genuine love for you. These are the people that have your back no matter what!

Serve Others: Serving others means to do things for other people. It's an attitude that says that you want to help others not out of a "look at me" motivation, but out of a desire to benefit the other person. Serving others is what true ministry is all about. I define *ministry* as simply meeting a need in the love of Jesus. Therefore, serving in essence is meeting the needs of other people with the love of Jesus. And so it comes as no surprise that this was the very attitude of Christ. He said in Matthew that He did not come to be served, but to serve by giving His very life for us all.

Not so with you. Instead, whoever wants to become great among you must be your servant, and whoever wants to be first must be your slave—just as the Son of Man did not come to be served, but to serve, and to give his life as a ransom for many. —Matthew 20: 26–28, niv

As a disciple of Christ, we are to follow His example in respect to our attitude of serving others. And trust me when I tell you, your church will have tons of areas where they will need your help. I can remember that when I first got saved my excitement for Jesus saving my life spilled over into my serving (and still does passionately to this day). When I finally found my "home" church, I wanted to do something, anything to serve God. One Sunday a pastor announced a need for ushers, and I signed up right away. I stayed faithful to ushering and then an opportunity was presented for Melanie and me to serve in the six through twelve-year-old area of the Children's Ministry. I was able to stay committed to both areas because I was ushering only one Sunday a month and it was great. Let me tell you, I loved it!

A few years passed and next thing I knew, we were promoted to associate youth pastors, serving the youth and overseeing the six through twelve-year-old area of the Children's Ministry—the very area we served in as volunteers for about two and a half years. This lasted for a season and then God promoted us again, but this time as head youth pastors running the youth ministry (ages thirteen through eighteen). That's how I found my "call" in ministry. It wasn't by sitting on the couch saying, "Past me a doughnut." Nope, it was by serving.

I want to tell you something that is very important about having a willingness to serve. When you are serving others, even though that person or people are benefiting, it is really unto the Lord. What you do for other people is for God (Matt. 25:40). You do it out of your love for God and His people. When you help them, you are serving God. Always remember that. We are God's servants!

Lastly, when choosing a church, pray and ask God to send you to the right one for you. One that will pass the Truth Test (See Chapter 5) with flying colors and where you will really receive what you need to grow spiritually in your relationship with God.

Now that I have Jesus, does that mean that life is going to be easy?

Now that you've received Jesus, does that mean that life is going to just be easy all of sudden and all the problems you had will just go away? No! This doesn't mean that life is just going to be "peaches and cream" from here on out because life is just life, and you will have tough times regardless. However, now you have a God who has promised to never leave nor forsake you (Josh. 1:5). You have a best friend who will give you peace in the middle of your troubles and the things you face in life. Jesus will help you get through the tough times while working it out for your benefit (Rom. 8:28). Through Christ, you will become more than you ever dreamed of being. I love you so much, and more importantly, God loves you. Welcome to the family of God! I'm telling you, it's the coolest family to be in and I'm so glad that you are now a part of it!

Chapter 7

That Night

It was July of 1996 and I was back in my hometown in Southern California on summer break after completing my third year of college in Pittsburgh. I remember that week like it was yesterday. I had just finished my summer internship for my field of study (at the time) and I was looking forward to just kicking back for that last week or two before I had to return to school. I contacted one of my friends that I grew up with and that night we went out to a club. Back in those days I used to smoke weed from time to time when I was partying and that night wasn't any different. I remember being in the club, high but yet still very aware of my surroundings.

At one point, I told my friend that I would be right back as I approached the dance floor to ask someone to dance. On my way, I was cut off by a woman wearing a red dress. What was strange about it was that she seemed to come out of nowhere. She crossed right in front of me while asking the question, "Why are you wandering?" Now when she said it the first time, I didn't get it. But when she asked me, "Why are you wandering" the second time, I got it! I don't know how I knew what she meant, I just did. She was talking about me wandering in a spiritual sense. I was wandering because I didn't have God in my life. I didn't have Jesus and as a result, I was lost, aimlessly wandering, that's what she meant.

Immediately, I felt a peace unlike any peace I had every felt before. At that very moment, in the middle of that club, I knew I was in the presence of God. This woman was an angel sent by God who looked and talked like a regular person. Also as a quick side note, God later confirmed my experience by leading me to a scripture that I didn't know anything about at the time: "Do not forget to entertain strangers, for by so doing some people have entertained angels without knowing it" (Heb. 13:2).

The angel began to tell me how much God loves me. She also said that I had such a good heart, but that if I continued in my wicked ways, I was going to reap what I sowed. Now you have to understand something. In my mind, I was a good person. I was going to college trying to better myself. I wasn't this person out killing people that they talked about on the news. I was the kind of person who would walk the little old lady across the street if she needed it. But the angel said to me, "If I, (me, "good person" Kelvin) continued in my wicked ways, I would reap what I sowed." In that moment, I looked around and I could "see" for the first time in my life. I could see that no matter how much of a "good person" I thought I was, I had a one-way ticket to hell without Jesus Christ. I realized that I was a sinner, living in sin. And as I visually scanned the club, I kept thinking: "I bet that all of these people here are just as empty inside as I am."

I recognized that there was no middle ground with God. He had given me a gift, His Son, Jesus, and I had either rejected Him or accepted Him. There was no "riding the fence." In fact, I realized that by not accepting Jesus I was in actuality rejecting Him. So, to break it down, my failure to make a decision to receive Christ before that night had become an automatic choice of rejecting Him. It was as if I had been wearing dark sunglasses (spiritually speaking) all of my life and God basically came along and in that moment took them off and said, "Here, this is the truth about your life and where you are headed." I was "deceived." Let me explain. When God took what I refer to as my "dark sunglasses" off and allowed me to see my state of reality, I also realized that because I was not serving God, I was living for Satan, the devil, without even knowing it. The deception was that I never thought in a million years of myself as a "devil worshiper" or anything like that.

However, it was really clear to me in that moment that I was either on God's side or the devil's side. There was no "middle" lifestyle option. I was in bondage to Satan without even knowing it. He had been influencing my whole life from the beginning even down to the music I listened too, everything! It was crazy! Also in that moment, the angel began to bring up some of the things that I had said to God and questions that I had asked Him throughout my childhood and early adulthood. It was as though God was finishing the conversation from years of my hearing nothing back. He was answering many of my thoughts and questions in that moment. He stated that I would help change a part of the world. (I have always felt in my heart, even as a child that in some way I wanted to help other people around the world. Things like aiding disadvantaged children and so forth.)

You see I was the type of person who always believed that God existed because you could go outside and just notice all of creation and know that God had to have created all of that. However, I didn't believe that He was real for me because when I talked to Him, I never heard anything back. Even when I heard more about Him later in my upbringing, I still didn't truly believe. I was the type of person that would say, "I'll believe it when I see it!" I never believed in God enough to surrender my life to Him. But that night in the club changed all of that. I couldn't deny what I was experiencing; it really happened. I remember even pinching myself that night because it seemed too good to be true. But the fact was that it wasn't a dream, it was really happening.

God was showing me that He was really real! I also remember that while the angel was talking to me, she kept having these serious expressions and gestures of deep concern mixed with compassion. She also kept saying that I would never see her again (like a warning to me). She had a serious, and I do mean serious, sense of urgency. The gestures were like, "I hope you're listening, the bomb is about to blow and you must get out to be saved, hurry!" After she finished her last sentence, the club lights came back on as my friend waved to me to come over to him. With weed smoke all over my black leather coat, I gave her a hug and said, "I've been listening to everything you have said and I'm going to change." She responded with a huge smile and a look of relief.

After I finished hugging her, I glanced at my friend and looked back (all within one second) and she was gone. I knew that there was no way somebody could leave that fast. It was as though she just vanished into thin air! I got in the car with my friend and his cousin in complete shock (in a good way) and didn't say anything to them about what had happened. Why? Because I didn't think they would believe me. I mean, I'm not sure I would have believed me if I were them and it hadn't happened to me.

After I got home, I remember feeling compelled to get on my knees. It was as though I felt a sense of awe of a presence greater than I had ever known that literally compelled me to bow down. So, on my knees (still with my black leather coat on and smelling like weed), I prayed to God. I said, "Lord, I see that you are real. If you can do anything with me, do it. I surrender." That was it. And let me tell you, that was the summer of 1996 and my life has never been the same!! God, through our relationship, has taken me through a process of change and filled my life with joy and purpose. He has led me on this path of destiny that He already had planned for me before the beginning of time as we know it! If you haven't already, join me. If He could do it we me, trust me when I tell you, He can do it with you.

Let me say this before I go. The thing that really broke me down to tears that night was not the whole heaven and hell thing (as real as it is). It was the fact that God loved me so much. I mean, He already knew about all of my "mess" and all about the "skeletons in my closet" before He came to me, but none of that mattered. That night, I felt His overwhelming unconditional love beyond any human capacity to love, and that love broke me down. I love Him so much because He first loved me! Again, if you have not already, I urge you to receive His love today. Don't wait another second; today is the day of salvation for you!

> For I am not ashamed of the gospel, for it is the power of God for salvation to everyone who believes (Rom 1:16).

I'm Telling the Truth! RECAP

Telling the Truth #1
God loves everybody the same, no matter what.

Telling the Truth #2
The kind of love that God has for us is the kind of love that would give up your life to be killed for someone who doesn't even know you.

Telling the Truth #3
You can't get into heaven on your own terms, you have to do it God's way.

Telling the Truth #4
Jesus died on the cross and was resurrected (raised from the dead) so we could be forgiven of our sins and receive eternal life.

Telling the Truth #5
Salvation is not earned, it is a free gift of God's grace.

Telling the Truth #6
I am right (in perfect standing) with God through faith in Jesus Christ *alone*.

Telling the Truth #7
Jesus is God.

Telling the Truth #8
Jesus is the Lamb of God.

Telling the Truth #9
Jesus is the Son of God.

Telling the Truth #10
Jesus is the Messiah.

Telling the Truth #11
Jesus is the *only way* to receive eternal life.

Telling the Truth #12
All I have to do to be saved and receive eternal life is believe in Jesus.

Bibliography

Definitions noted, Merriam-Webster Online Dictionary, are from the Merriam-Webster Online Dictionary. Copyright © 2005 by Merriam-Webster, Incorporation.

Definitions noted, The New International Webster's Standard Dictionary, are from The New International Webster's Standard Dictionary. Copyright © 2006 by Trident Reference Publishing.

Notes

Chapter 1

What's the Gospel?

1. The NAS New Testament Greek Lexicon (from www. crosswalk.com), s.v. "fears" (to reverence) in Acts 10:35. See section entitled: "God loves me the same, no matter what culture I am from," on page 7 of the manuscript.

2. The New International Webster's Standard Dictionary. Copyright © 2006 by Trident Reference Publishing. Citation-definition for venerate: to regard with respect or awe. Please note that venerate was another word provided by The NAS New Testament Greek Lexicon (from www.crosswalk.com) for the s.v. "fears" in Acts 10:35. Venerate was included with the definition "to reverence." To make it easy for my reader, I simply provided the definition of venerate so that the reference reads: "the person who fears [to reverence; to regard with respect or awe] Him and does what is right is welcome to Him." Also see section entitled: "God loves me the same, no matter what culture I am from," on page seven of the manuscript.

3. Holman Bible Dictionary. Copyright © 1991 by Holman Bible Publishers. See pages 10-12 of the manuscript under the section entitled: "What is a crucifixion? And what exactly happened to a person being crucified?" The facts about the method of crucifixion is based on my study of the information provided by this dictionary.

Chapter 4

Who Is Jesus?

1. Holman Bible Dictionary. Copyright © 1991 by

Holman Bible Publishers. See page 45 of the manuscript under the section entitled, "The Truth #9: Jesus is the Messiah." The citation includes the transliteration of the word *Messiah* in the Hebrew language (translated: "anointed one") and the Greek language (translated: "Christos"). These definitions and the information provided about the coming of the Messiah, based on Jewish history, were provided by this dictionary.

To Contact the Author

Kelvin would love to hear from you.

Did you receive Jesus as a result of reading this book?

Do you have a story or testimony that you would like to share?

Would you like to invite Kelvin to speak to your group or at your event?

If so, please visit our Web site for the most current mailing address and contact information:

Web site: www.theocwebsite.com

You may also e-mail us at: ocministry@live.com